Jesus and the Marginalized
in John's Gospel

Zacchaeus Studies: New Testament

General Editor: Mary Ann Getty

Jesus and the Marginalized in John's Gospel

by

Robert J. Karris, O.F.M.

A Michael Glazier Book
THE LITURGICAL PRESS
Collegeville, Minnesota

About the Author

Father Robert J. Karris, O.F.M. is Provincial Minister of the Franciscan Province of the Sacred Heart (St. Louis-Chicago). Educated at Catholic University (S.T.L.) and Harvard University (TH.D.), he was professor of New Testament Studies at Catholic Theological Union at Chicago from 1971-1987. In Fr. Karris's many publications, the topic of the poor and rich in the Gospels, especially in Luke, occupies pride of place.

A Michael Glazier Book
published by
THE LITURGICAL PRESS

Cover design by Maureen Daney. Typography by Mary Brown.

1	2	3	4	5	6	7	8	9

Library of Congress Cataloging-in-Publication Data

Karris, Robert J.
    Jesus and the marginalized in John's Gospel / by Robert J. Karris.
        p.   cm. — (Zacchaeus studies. New Testament)
    "A Michael Glazier book."
    Includes bibliographical references (p.)
    ISBN 0-8146-5774-5
    1. Bible. N.T. John—Criticism, interpretation, etc.
    2. Marginality, Social—Biblical teaching. 3. Sociology, Biblical.
    4. Jesus Christ—Teachings. I. Title. II. Series.
    BS2615.6.S55K37   1990
    226.5′08305568—dc20   89-7623
                                                  CIP

Contents

Dedicated To My Colleagues
In The Book And In The Land:
Carroll, Dianne, Don, Hayim
Jennifer, Leslie, and Lyn

Editor's Note

Zacchaeus Studies provide concise, readable and relatively inexpensive scholarly studies on particular aspects of scripture and theology. The New Testament section of the series presents studies dealing with focal or debated questions; and the volumes focus on specific texts of particular themes of current interest in biblical interpretation. Specialists have their professional journals and other forums where they discuss matters of mutual concern, exchange ideas and further contemporary trends of research; and some of their work on contemporary biblical research is now made accessible for students and others in *Zacchaeus Studies.*

The authors in this series share their own scholarship in non-technical language, in the areas of their expertise and interest. These writers stand with the best in current biblical scholarship in the English-speaking world. Since most of them are teachers, they are accustomed to presenting difficult material in comprehensible form without compromising a high level of critical judgment and analysis.

The works of this series are ecumenical in content and purpose and cross credal boundaries. They are designed to augment formal and informal biblical study and discussion. Hopefully they will also serve as texts to enhance and supplement seminary, university and college classes. The series will also aid Bible study groups, adult education and parish religious education classes to develop intelligent, versatile and challenging programs for those they serve.

Mary Ann Getty
New Testament Editor

Introduction

Each year for the past ten years I have taught a course on the Gospel of John and a course on the Gospel of Luke. Over these years I have written extensively on Luke and have focused my attention on its theme of rich and poor. During the last three years I have been consciously asking myself a question which was always in the back of my mind: why doesn't John have much, if anything, to say about the theme of rich and poor, which Luke develops in almost every chapter of his Gospel? In class preparation for John's Gospel these past three years I have scoured commentaries and other resources to ascertain whether anyone has written on this subject or even suggested that John might have something to say about this theme. My initial research indicated that little is written on this issue. The leisure of a sabbatical year has afforded me the opportunity to pursue this question at greater depth.

After checking through the recent bibliographies of Jürgen Becker (1986), James D. G. Dunn (1983), Robert Kysar (1983, 1985), and Stephen S. Smalley (1986) and after consulting works on liberation theology, I confirmed the impression my initial research had created: very little has been written on the subject of the rich and poor in John's Gospel. And what had been written was largely ignored in bibliographies. I refer here to the works of Frederick Herzog (1972), José Miranda (1977), and José Comblin (1979). For example, no one seemed to take seriously what Herzog (1971: 53) wrote about John 1:46: "Jesus himself belongs to the *marginales*, the forgotten, the nobodies.

It is exactly where the glory of humanity is least obvious that it appears in its true power. We dare never forget the identity of Jesus with the marginal figures of life."

I reflected that if so many mainline scholars had not adverted to or seen this theme in John's Gospel, the reason may be that the theme does not exist in his version of the good news. But as the wags would say, such an answer would put me out of a job or, better yet, give me time on my sabbatical to journey to far away places and relax a spell. But I thought to myself, how can John's Gospel be gospel if he omits what theologians, general chapters of religious institutes, episcopal conferences, and Vatican pronouncements are terming a constitutive element of the gospel, namely, Jesus' preferential option for the poor? (See the excursus at the end of this Introduction for some salient ecclesiastical quotations.) I questioned some more. Might the negative results of scholarly research on the presence of this theme in John's Gospel provide armaments for critics of liberation theology? For they might muse that the so-called preferential option for the poor cannot be a constitutive element of the gospel if one of the major gospels—some would even say *the* major gospel—does not have much, if anything, on that thematic.

My thoughts continued. Might John have so little to say to us about Jesus and the poor because we come to him with ears trained to hear Jesus as Matthew, Mark, and Luke present him? And since John does not contain Matthew's parable about the sheep and the goats and Mark's story about the rich young man and Luke's account of Jesus' inaugural sermon at Nazareth—key passages today for identifying a gospel as one which proclaims good news to the poor—John's Gospel is judged on this Synoptic scale and found wanting. May it be that John has his own way, his own idiom for dealing with this thematic?

My thoughts spiraled further. Might the very category of "Jesus and the poor" have prevented scholars from seeing how John actually deals with the reality that scholarly category is trying to illumine? For example, Jon Sobrino (1984: 136-137) illumines the Synoptic Gospel materials on the poor quite well by employing the scholarly category of "Jesus and the poor." He makes a helpful distinction between social poverty, spiritual poverty which means a basic openness to the spirit of God, and metaphysical poverty which is correlative to and inherent in the limited condition of every human being. But when he discusses what social poverty means in the concrete, one will look in vain for mention of the oppression of women, which was prevalent during New Testament times. This example illustrates that the net provided by the scholarly category of "Jesus and the poor" is not fine enough to capture an important aspect of the reality of Jesus' ministry, namely, his liberation of oppressed women, an aspect which is so pervasive in John's Gospel. The following observations of Elisabeth Schüssler Fiorenza further opened my eyes to the deficiencies of the scholarly category of "Jesus and the poor":

> Moreover, I do not think that the social category of 'the poor' is sufficient to describe the inclusive character of the Jesus movement. Added to this category must be that of 'the marginal,' because the healing stories, as well as the descriptions of other persons in the Jesus traditions, indicate that Jesus and his movement were open to all, especially to the 'outcast' of his society and religion. Although the majority of the tax collectors, prostitutes, and sinners might have been poor, some of them probably were not.

While the terminology Fiorenza uses is largely drawn from the Synoptic Gospels and deals with the movement initiated by Jesus of Nazareth, her remarks are very helpful for our study of John's Gospel and its christological portrait of Jesus of Nazareth. As we will see, John's Gospel does deal somewhat with those who are "poor" and "rich." But the category of "Jesus and the poor" will not allow us to see the full dimension of Jesus' mission in John's Gospel. To detect that dimension we need the category of "Jesus and the marginalized." This category will include those who are made marginal because they do not know the law (7:49), those who are marginal because they are not Jews, but Samaritans (4:4-42), those who are marginal because they are chronically ill (9:1-41), those who are marginal because they are women. In each instance "the marginal" person is being judged by some norm and found to be "outcast," "inferior," "of lower status." Thus, for example, the people of the land are inferior to the religious leaders who know the law (7:49); the Samaritan woman is inferior on two counts at least, for she is not from Judea and is a woman.

To bring my spiraling thoughts to a close, in the hermeneutical category of "Jesus and the marginalized" I am convinced that I have found the key to seeing in John's Gospel what others, myself included, have seen in the Synoptic Gospels and have called Jesus' preferential option for the poor. In this book I want to share my conviction with you, my readers, and persuade you of its rightness. In a sense, then, this book belongs to the category of a "*quaestio disputanda*," a question-to-be-disputed. I invite you to challenge and test my thesis, which is: John's Gospel has much to contribute to any discussion of Jesus' ministry to those who are on the fringes of society and of religion.

In the chapters which follow I will argue my case thematically rather than proceed through John's Gospel chapter by chapter. Chapter 1 will deal with questions of method. Chapter 2 will be taken up with what John has to say about alms to the poor. Chapters 3, 4, 5, and 6 will be specifically devoted to "the marginals" in John's Gospel. The people of the land, who are ignorant of the Law, will be featured in Chapter 3. Chapter 4 will discuss the physically afflicted. Chapter 5 will focus on a male and female "marginal," the royal official and the Samaritan woman. Chapter 6 will explore the remaining female characters in John's Gospel. Chapter 7 will focus on Nicodemus, a marginalizer, who becomes a disciple. Chapter 8 will bring together the suggestions about the life situation of John's community, which I have made in Chapters 2-7, and will also probe the impact the evangelist's response to his life situation has on our contemporary life situation. A selected bibliography will complete the volume.

I envision my audience as those who have had a recent foundational course in New Testament and who have mastered a basic commentary on John's Gospel like that of James McPolin (1982) in the New Testament Message Series from Michael Glazier, Inc.

All biblical quotations are based on the Revised Standard Version.

Excursus: Ecclesiastical Documentation on Preferential Option for the Poor

I give the documentation in chronological order and italicize key words or phrases for easy crossreferencing.

1971 SYNOD OF CATHOLIC BISHOPS

Action on behalf of justice and participation in the transformation of the world fully appear to us as *a constitutive dimension of the preaching of the Gospel*, or, in other words, of the Church's mission for the redemption of the human race and its liberation from every oppressive situation (#6 of "Justice in the World," Synod of Bishops, Second General Assembly, November 30, 1971; quoted from p. 514 of Joseph Gremillion, presenter, *The Gospel of Peace and Justice: Catholic Social Teaching since Pope John* [Maryknoll: Orbis, 1976]).

EVANGELIZATION IN LATIN AMERICA'S PRESENT AND FUTURE, final document of the Third General Conference of the Latin American Episcopate, Puebla, Mexico, 1979. Part IV, Chapter 1 deals with "A Preferential Option for the Poor" (#1128-1165):

With renewed hope in the vivifying power of the Spirit, we are going to take up once again the position of the Second General Conference of the Latin American episcopate in Medellin, which adopted a clear and *prophetic option expressing preference for, and solidarity with, the poor*. We do this despite the distortions and interpretations of some, who vitiate the spirit of Medellin, and despite the disregard and even hostility of others (OAP: Intro.). We affirm the need for conversion on the part of the whole Church to a preferential option for the poor, an option aimed at their integral liberation (#1134).

Commitment to the poor and oppressed and the rise of grassroots communities have helped the Church to discover the evangelizing potential of the poor. For the poor challenge the Church constantly, summoning it to conversion; and many of the poor incarnate in their lives the evangelical values of solidarity, service, simplicity, and openness to accepting the gift of God (1147). (*Puebla and Beyond: Documentation and Commentary.* Ed. John Eagleson and Philip Scharper; Maryknoll: Orbis, 1979.)

NATIONAL CONFERENCE OF CATHOLIC BISH-OPS, November 13, 1986—"Economic Justice for All: Catholic Social Teaching and the U.S. Economy"

Such (biblical) perspectives provide a basis for what today is called the *'preferential option for the poor.'* Though in the Gospels and in the New Testament as a whole the offer of salvation is extended to all peoples, Jesus takes the side of those most in need, physically and spiritually. The example of Jesus poses a number of challenges to the contemporary church. It imposes a prophetic mandate to speak for those who have no one to speak for them, to be a defender of the defenseless, who in biblical terms are the poor. It also demands a compassionate vision that enables the church to see things from the side of the poor and powerless, and to assess lifestyle, policies and social institutions in terms of their impact on the poor. It summons the church also to be an instrument in assisting people to experience the liberating power of God in their own lives, so that they may respond to the Gospel in freedom and in dignity. Finally, and most radically, it calls for an emptying of self, both individually and corporately, that allows the church to experience the power of God in the midst of poverty and powerlessness (#52).

As individuals and as a nation, therefore, we are called to

make a fundamental 'option for the poor.' The obligation
to evaluate social and economic activity from the viewpoint
of the poor and the powerless arises from the radical com-
mand to love one's neighbor as one's self. Those who are
marginalized and whose rights are denied have privileged
claims if society is to provide justice for all. This obligation
is deeply rooted in Christian belief. As Paul VI stated: In
teaching us charity, the Gospel instructs us in the preferential
respect due the poor and the special situation they have in
society: the more fortunate should renounce some of their
rights so as to place their goods more generously at the
service of others. John Paul II has described this special
obligation to the poor as 'a call to have a special openness
with the small and the weak, those that suffer and weep,
those that are humiliated and left on the *margin of society*,
so as to help them win their dignity as human persons and
children of God.' The prime purpose of this special commitment to the poor is to enable them to become active par-
ticipants in the life of society. It is to enable all persons to
share in and contribute to the common good. The 'option
for the poor,' therefore, is not an adversarial slogan that pits
one group or class against another. Rather it states that the
deprivation and powerlessness of the poor wounds the whole
community. The extent of their suffering is a measure of
how far we are from being a true community of persons.
These wounds will be healed only by greater solidarity with
the poor and among the poor themselves (87-88).

1

Preliminaries

Our discussion, in the Introduction, of the scholarly categories of "Jesus and the poor" and "Jesus and the marginalized" set the stage for this chapter. In it we will deal with three more preliminary and methodological matters. The first one is simply put. In chapters one through seven I will draw my data from the Gospel of John. It is only in chapter eight below that data from the Epistles of John will be introduced as I endeavor to reconstruct a life situation or *Sitz im Leben* to account for the Johannine community's teachings on Jesus and the marginalized. The remaining two preliminary items will take more space to develop.

A Concordance Study Will Not Give the Total Picture

From our discussion of the category of "Jesus and the marginalized" in the Introduction readers may have drawn the legitimate conclusion that we are dealing with a rich and multi-dimensional theme. A mere concordance study of the occurrence of the words "poor" or "rich" is insufficient to detect the presence of this thematic in a Gospel. Readers must attend to a Gospel's story line of how Jesus relates to various people and how they relate to one another to detect this theme.

To give a Synoptic example, Jesus' curing of the woman with the flow of blood in Mark 5:25-34 is rightly seen as Jesus' liberation of a poor and marginalized person by Elisabeth

Schüssler Fiorenza although the actual words "poor" and "marginalized" nowhere occur in this passage. She writes:

> 'She had spent all that she had' by consulting 'many physicians' but 'she was not better but rather grew worse.' These few terse words *narrate* forcefully the economic impoverishment of the incurably ill. However, this woman's predicament was not just incurable illness but also permanent uncleanness. She was not only unclean herself, but polluted everyone and everything with which she came in contact (Lev 15:19-31). For twelve years this women had been 'polluted' and barred from the congregation of the 'holy people.' No wonder she risked financial ruin and economic destitution to become healthy, and therefore cultically clean, again (1983: 124; emphasis mine).

Indeed, the evangelists will deal with Jesus' care of the poor in narrative or story form without using the word for "poor." A simple glance at a concordance under the word "poor" is not sufficient to reveal the depth and breadth of this theme in a Gospel. Indeed, evangelists, John included, will narrate how laws of ritual cleanliness have marginalized people, like the woman with the flow of blood, away from the life of the community without ever using the word "marginalized."

To take a Johannine example, a first reading of John 9:1-41 and a concordance study of its terminology may not reveal how this masterpiece of John's theology and artistry relates to his theme of Jesus and the marginalized. Our eyes, often trained to see baptismal overtones in this story of how a person gradually comes to faith in Jesus, are not so keen on seeing this chronically ill person as a beggar who is on the fringes of society. But the evangelist does portray him in 9:8 as a "beggar" (*prosaitēs*). Furthermore, as we will see in greater detail in chapter four below, the story line shows how the blind beggar is marginalized by the religious leaders who judge him by the norm of whether he knows the law of Moses. These leaders, who are disciples of Moses, judge that the beggar who now sees is ignorant of the law. They shove him to the margins of their religious society and even cast him out of the synagogue

(9:34). But this beggar, who has lost his moorings in synagogue life and society, is welcomed by Jesus.

Close scrutiny of John's stories will reward us with more contributions to our theme of Jesus and the marginalized than any number of concordance studies.

Let John Be John!

Another methodological caution has to do with our tendency to harmonize the Gospels. All of us, even the most sophisticated New Testament scholars among us, have a proclivity to blend together aspects from the four gospels into one story. That harmonized version is so powerful that at times it can prevent us from reading a Gospel for what it has to say in its own right. For example, it may be quite difficult for us to hear John 19:38-42 aright because the tape of harmonization that sounds in our mind's ear is that of the Synoptics. In the Synoptic account of Jesus' burial Joseph of Arimathea is a solitary figure. In John's Gospel, however, he is accompanied by Nicodemus, who has been featured earlier in 3:1-21 and 7:50-52 and who is now described in 19:39 as a rich man who brings an extraordinarily large amount of spices—100 pounds—for Jesus' burial. It seems to me that our unconscious tendency is not to hear what John says about Nicodemus because he doesn't fit into our harmonized version. But more about rich Nicodemus in chapter seven below.

Stereotypes of Jesus and his disciples, derived from the Synoptics, may also prevent us from hearing John on his own wavelength. Although contemporary scholarship tells us that Jesus and his first disciples were probably middle-class artisans, many of us continue to have a stereotype of Jesus and his band as being poor. Our stereotype continues. Jesus' first followers gave up their meager possessions to follow Jesus and were cared for by the people. They had no money of their own. If the tape of these stereotypes plays in your mind's ears, you may be surprised, as I was, to hear John's Gospel saying that Jesus and his disciples not only had money, but also had a systematic way of handling their money. Their money box apparently contained more than two hundred days' wages, and they used some of their money to care for the poor. But we are ahead of ourselves. I will provide more on this point in a later discussion about John 12:1-8; 13:29; 6:5-8 in chapter two below.

A homely example will illustrate my point about "Let John Be John!" Some time ago I learned of the death of a friend. The first report I heard said that my friend had been brutally mugged in a New York City subway. His assailants had stripped him of wallet, watch, and ring. He had died en route to the hospital. Some four days later I heard the definitive version of my friend's last hours. He had suffered a severe heart attack in a New York City subway and had badly bruised his face against a pillar as he fell. Standers-by made off with his valuables. He was dead on arrival at the hospital. As I later told mutual friends about his death, I found myself about to tell the story according to the first tape. It took a conscious and strong effort to override that tape with the factual version. That first report had so impressed itself on my mind that the definitive version had a hard time being heard. Something similar may happen to all of us as we try to hear anew what John has to say about Jesus and the marginalized. The first report will continue to say to us: John has nothing, or at best, little to say on this theme. It will take a concerted effort on our part just to hear another version of the data, let alone accord that version definitive or factual status. Patient listening is the first step towards a sound cure for "harmonizing-itis." Let John Be John!

Conclusion

In the chapters that follow I will explore other dimensions of the theme of Jesus and the marginalized in John's Gospel and will do so employing the methodology I have set forth in this chapter.

My goal in this study is not to argue that my way of reading John's stories is the only way, but to point relentlessly my readers' attention to the presence of the theme of Jesus and the

marginalized in John's Gospel. I do not maintain that this
theme is the only one in John's stories or the most important.
My contention is that this theme does exist in John's Gospel,
has not been given sufficient attention, and should be heard
for what it has to contribute to the contemporary issue of
Jesus' and the Church's preferential option for the outcasts of
society and religion.

2

Alms to the Poor

We will begin our exploration of the Johannine theme of "Jesus and the marginalized" by examining John's four explicit references to "the poor." After discussing these references, which occur in 12:5-8 and 13:29 and deal with giving alms to the poor, we will take a brief look at a related passage, 6:5-8. We will conclude with suggestions about John's life situation.

It is vital to recall, at the beginning of this chapter, that giving alms to the poor was part of normative Jewish piety. The normative character of this practice is well illustrated in Matthew's Sermon on the Mount, in which Matthew adopts this foundation of Jewish life after purifying it of its abuses. The Matthean Jesus teaches:

> Beware of practicing your piety before men and women in order to be seen by them; for then you will have no reward from your Father who is in heaven. Thus, when you give alms, sound no trumpet before you, as the hypocrites do in the synagogues and in the streets, that they may be praised by men and women. Truly, I say to you, they have their reward. But when you give alms, do not let your left hand know what your right hand is doing, so that your alms may be in secret; and your Father who sees in secret will reward you (Matt 6:1-4).

The commentary which W.D. Davies (1964: 308) provides on Matt 6:1-4 confirms for us the normative character of almsgiving for Judaism. Moreover, in his observations about the life situation of Matthew's community, Davies may also illumine that of John's community. Could it be that both communities had to react to the almsgiving initiatives of Pharisaic Judaism as that movement was reorganizing itself at Jamnia after the Jewish War of A.D. 66-70? But we are ahead of ourselves. More on John's life situation at the end of this chapter. Here is what Davies says about Matt 6:1-4 and Matthew's community:

> Has the priority given by Matthew to almsgiving in vi. 2ff. any significance? For obvious reasons, arising out of post-war conditions, almsgiving was given a special prominence in Jamnian Judaism: its regulation was of serious concern to the Sages. It may be objected that, ideally at least, concern for the poor had always been a mark of Judaism, and that it is, therefore, illegitimate to insist upon it as characteristic of the Jamnian period. Nevertheless, although the depression of Jewry after A.D. 70 has sometimes been over-emphasized, the economic condition of most was such that only an extraordinary effort at philanthropy on the part of the more fortunate ones could avail to preserve the nation ... Possibly in the Matthaean community similar factors were at work.

Our appetites whetted by Davies' commentary, we are now in a position to see how John handles the Jewish norm of giving alms to the poor. As we have cautioned in chapter one, we must be prepared to let John surprise us. "Let John Be John!"

JOHN 12:5-8
THE MONEY OF JESUS AND HIS DISCIPLES
IS FOR ALMSGIVING

Although we will be concerned primarily with 12:5-8, it will be helpful to quote the entire Johannine story of Jesus' anointing (12:1-8). Readers should bear in mind that the roles which

Martha and Mary have in this story and the contrast between generous Mary and greedy Judas will be examined below in chapter six on Women in John's Gospel.

> [1]Six days before the Passover, Jesus came to Bethany, where Lazarus was, whom Jesus had raised from the dead. [2]There they made him a supper; Martha served, and Lazarus was one of those at table with him. [3]Mary took a pound of costly ointment of pure nard and anointed the feet of Jesus and wiped his feet with her hair; and the house was filled with the fragrance of the ointment. [4]But Judas Iscariot, one of his disciples (he who was to betray him), said, [5]'Why was this ointment not sold for three hundred denarii and given to the poor?' [6]This he said, not that he cared for the poor but because he was a thief, and as he had the money box he used to take what was put into it. [7]Jesus said, 'Let her alone, let her keep it for the day of my burial. [8]The poor you always have with you, but you do not always have me.'

Before addressing the major exegetical concerns of this passage, we must identify and combat a tape, which plays in countless minds and conveys a misinterpretation of our passage, especially of 12:8. This tape proclaims that even Jesus said that you cannot eliminate poverty. This misinterpretation is exampled in the jargon of critics of social welfare programs, who glibly observe that even Jesus taught that you cannot eliminate the poor as a class in society; they will always be with us. Unless we attend to this tape, its false message may prevent us from hearing 12:1-8 aright. Pheme Perkins (1978: 133) corrects this misuse of 12:8: "Jesus' saying, then, does not reject the principle of concern for the poor; he merely rejects the attempt to invoke it against the woman." While Perkins' interpretation is surely correct and while you and I may be convinced by it, those two factors do not mean that we have thereby erased the tape which plays in our minds and in the minds of countless others. Unless we attend to that tape and consciously record over its incorrect message, we may never adequately hear what John is saying in 12:5-8.

Now that we have alerted ourselves to the tape of "preserve

the status quo" which may play in our minds' ears when we hear 12:8, we can attend to the rest of John 12:1-8 and the contributions it makes to our study. First, John 12:5,6,8 contain three of the four instances of the Greek word used by the Synoptics for "poor" (*ptōchos;* this word is used in various contexts five times in Matthew, five times in Mark, and ten times in Luke). The only other instance of "the poor" in John occurs in his account of Jesus' last meal with his disciples (13:29). In 13:29, too, Judas and the care of the poor is at issue. Benedetto Prete (1978: 443-44) calls attention to this concentrated use of alms for "the poor" in John 12:5, 6, 8; 13:29 and suggests that in these chapters we may have a compendium of John's teachings on "the poor." What meaning John ascribes to this "compendium" will be seen in our next point.

John contains two items of information about Judas not found in the Synoptics. It is Judas who asks the question in 12:5: "Why was this ointment not sold for three hundred denarii and given to the poor?" In Matt 26:8-9 it is the disciples who ask a similar question. In Mark 14:4-5 it is "some" who ask this question. At this point, for the sake of making some sense out of the sum of "three hundred denarii," I will pause and convert this ancient monetary sum into U.S. dollars. Now the denarius was a day's wage. Taking as norms the minimum wage of $3.35 an hour and a day's work at eight hours, we figure that a day's wage is $26.80. If we multiply that amount by 300, we conclude that the ointment was worth $8,040. Let us now return to our second new piece of information about Judas. John's Gospel is alone in saying: "This Judas said, not that *he cared for* the poor (*ouch hoti peri tōn ptōchon emelen autō*) but because he was a thief, and as he had the money box he used to take what was put into it" (12:6). In penning 12:6, John has used the same Greek formula he employed in his description of the hireling in 10:13: "He flees because he is a hireling and *cares* nothing *for* the sheep (*ou melei autō peri tōn probatōn*)." Thus, John depicts Judas as a self-serving individual.

Let us pause and reflect further on the meaning of our second observation. It seems clear to me that John is saying that Judas was the treasurer of the monies which Jesus and his disciples possessed. It also seems clear that 12:5-6 presuppose that some of the monies given into the money box of Jesus and his band would be used as alms for the poor. As Rudolf Bultmann (1971: 415 n. 8) sagaciously remarks: "It is then presupposed that the disciple group receives and distributes gifts for the poor, hence perhaps the custom reflected in Acts 4.37 or in later church use." Thus, in John's view Jesus and his disciples own money, some of which they give to the poor.

It is vitally important that we dwell some more on the implications of our second observation. What John's Gospel says about Jesus and his first disciples goes against the stereotypes we have inherited from the Synoptics. These stereotypes tell us that Jesus and his disciples had nowhere to lay their heads, had no money, and were cared for by women. It is the Synoptic Jesus who tells his would-be disciples to sell their possessions and give them as alms to the poor and then follow him. It is the Johannine Jesus, on the other hand, who, along with his disciples, has money and gives alms to the poor. As I insisted in chapter one, we have to get into deep contact with our stereotypes and tapes and not let them prevent us from hearing what John has to say. Let John Be John!

In chapter eight below we will explore in depth John's life situation or *Sitz im Leben*. For now I raise the question of whether John's stress on Jesus' and his disciples' care of the poor stems from his desire to depict them as abiding by genuine Jewish norms. And this Johannine picture of Jesus and his disciples as almsgivers is all the more remarkable when one notes that in John's Gospel there is a systematic replacement by Jesus of Jewish traditions, institutions, and feasts. For example, Jesus' new wine replaces the water of purification (2:1-11); Jesus replaces the Temple (2:12-25). And yet John's Gospel portrays Jesus as observing the Jewish norm of giving alms. For John and his community that norm, while all others may be transformed, remains.

JOHN 13:29
JESUS AND HIS DISCIPLES USE
THEIR MONEY FOR ALMSGIVING

It is not necessary to quote all of John 13 in order to set the context for our next passage. John 13:21, 26-30 will suffice:

> [21]When Jesus had thus spoken, he was troubled in spirit, and testified, 'Truly, truly, I say to you, one of you will betray me.' . . . [26]Jesus answered, 'It is he to whom I shall give this morsel when I have dipped it.' So when he had dipped the morsel, he gave it to Judas, the son of Simon Iscariot. [27]Then after the morsel, Satan entered into him. Jesus said to him, 'What you are going to do, do quickly.' [28]Now no one at the table knew why he said this to him. [29]Some thought that, because Judas had the money box, Jesus was telling him, 'Buy what we need for the feast'; or, that he should give something to the poor. [30]So, after receiving the morsel, he immediately went out; and it was night.

Since we have given detailed comments above on 12:5-8 and how Judas was to give alms to the poor from the money box of Jesus and his disciples, there is no need to devote much space to 13:29. For this passage merely confirms what we already know from 12:5-8: Jesus and his disciples used some of their money to care for the poor. Two observations will suffice.

Over the last four years intensive work has been done on John's extensive use of irony. Therefore, it should come as no surprise that irony may be involved in 13:29 and 12:5-8. Here is what R. Alan Culpepper (1983: 174) says:

> Judas protests the waste of precious ointment at the proleptic anointment of Jesus for his burial, yet Judas bears a heavy share of responsibility for that burial. His pretense is concern for the poor, but he was pilfering from the common purse (12:4-6). Then, by an irony of events, the other disciples think Judas has gone out to 'give something to the

poor' when he slips off into the night to betray Jesus (13:29).
From another vantage point one can see that he gave more
to the poor than they realized.

Culpepper's perceptions may well open up another dimension
of 13:29 and 12:5-8, but the ironic dimension of the passages
we are studying should not blind us to the reality which lies at
the base of John's irony: Judas, the greedy traitor, was the
keeper of the money box from which Jesus and his disciples
gave money to the poor.

Commentators, in interpreting 13:29, are wont to refer to
the research of Joachim Jeremias (1966: 54) concerning the
giving of alms to the poor on passover night. Jeremias' words
are worth repeating in this context: "*It was, however, cus-
tomary to do something for the poor on the passover night*"
(emphasis his). If this is true, our passage may again be
accentuating how observant of certain Jewish norms Jesus
and his disciples were.

In sum, an analysis of 13:29 has added another building
block in our case that in John Jesus and his disciples are
portrayed as using their money to give alms to the poor. They
would observe passover by following the Jewish norms of
giving alms to the poor.

JOHN 6:5-8
THE MONEY OF JESUS AND HIS DISCIPLES
IS USED TO SUPPLY FOR THE NEEDS OF OTHERS

From 12:5-8 and 13:29 we have learned that Jesus and his
disciples had money and used some of it to relieve the needs of
the poor. This fact may illumine the peculiarities of 6:5-8 in
John's account of the multiplication of the loaves. In order to
let these verses be truly heard in their own right, I will first
present the parallel verses from the Synoptic Gospels. As
readers work through the four accounts, they should pay
special attention to John's uniqueness. I will assist your per-
ception of John's uniqueness by italicizing the main features
of 6:5-8.

Matthew 14:14-17

> [14]As he went ashore he saw a great throng; and he had
> compassion on them, and healed their sick. [15]When it was
> evening, the disciples came to him and said, 'this is a lonely
> place, and the day is now over; send the crowds away to go
> into the villages and buy food for themselves.' [16]Jesus said,
> 'They need not go away; you give them something to eat.'
> [17]They said to him, 'We have only five loaves here and two
> fish.'

Mark 6:34-38

> [34]As he went ashore he saw a great throng, and he had
> compassion on them, because they were like sheep without
> a shepherd; and he began to teach them many things. [35]And
> when it grew late, his disciples came to him and said, 'This
> is a lonely place, and the hour is now late; [36]send them
> away, to go into the country and villages round about and
> buy themselves something to eat.' [37]But he answered them,
> 'You give them something to eat.' And they said to him,
> 'Shall we go and buy two hundred denarii worth of bread,
> and give it to them to eat?' [38]And he said to them, 'How
> many loaves have you? Go and see.' And when they had
> found out, they said, 'Five, and two fish.'

Luke 9:11-13

> [11]When the crowds learned it, they followed him; and he
> welcomed them and spoke to them of the kingdom of God,
> and cured those who had need of healing. [12]Now the day
> began to wear away; and the twelve came and said to him,
> 'Send the crowd away, to go into the villages and country
> round about, to lodge and get provisions; for we are here in
> a lonely place.' [13]But he said to them, 'You give them some-
> thing to eat.' They said, 'We have no more than five loaves
> and two fish—unless we are to go and buy food for all these
> people.'

John 6:3-9

³Jesus went up on the mountain, and there sat down with his disciples. ⁴Now the Passover, the feast of the Jews, was at hand. ⁵Lifting up his eyes, then, and seeing that a multitude was coming to him, *Jesus said to Philip, 'How are we to buy bread, so that these people may eat?'⁶This he said to test him, for he himself knew what he would do. ⁷Philip answered him,* 'Two hundred denarii would not buy enough bread for each of them to get a little.' ⁸One of his disciples, Andrew, Simon Peter's brother, said to him, ⁹"There is a lad here who has five barley loaves and two fish; but what are they among so many?'

A comparison of the four accounts reveals the following points. First, the Synoptics describe the disciples or the Twelve taking the initiative and telling Jesus to dismiss the crowd. In John Jesus takes the initiative (6:5). John will develop this feature at great length in the bread of life discourse which follows and interprets this sign. It is Jesus who satisfies human hunger. Second, unique to John is also Jesus' question in 6:5: "How are we to buy bread, so that these people may eat?" Let us expand on this unique feature a bit. If we assume, along with our deeply held stereotypes, that Jesus and his disciples did not have money, then the Johannine Jesus' question is surely a trick question. But what happens if we view 6:5 from the perspective of our previous analyses of 12:5-8 and 13:29? Readers will recall that we concluded from a study of those passages that Jesus and his disciples did have money and used some of it to care for the needy. Might Jesus' question in 6:5 be one based on the fact that there is money in the money box held by Judas, money which could be used to care for the needy hungry?

The third feature of this passage proper to John is 6:6, which says that Jesus was testing Philip. The fourth special Johannine feature is found in 6:7, wherein Philip insists that two-hundred days' wages worth of bread will not satisfy the crowd's needs. This is different from Mark 6:37, which seems to imply that two-hundred days' wages worth of bread would be sufficient. From these last two features we can ascertain the nature of Jesus' testing of Philip.   Jesus had asked Philip about the amount of money needed to feed the hungry. Philip had given a business manager's answer: we have money, but not the amount it would take to feed this crowd. The test, especially as seen from the perspective of the rest of John 6, focuses on this question: Will the disciples and the crowd trust in Jesus to provide food which truly satisfies or will they trust in something else—money?

In conclusion to my analysis of John 6:5-8, my point is simple: this passage is related to 12:5-8 and 13:29 in that it, too, indicates that Jesus and his disciples had money which they used to care for needy people. Jesus' question to Philip in 6:5 makes sense on one level because the disciples do have the monetary wherewithal to buy some bread for the needy hungry. It does not make sense on another level—and here we are face to face with Johannine misunderstanding—because money alone, although vitally important for life, will not satisfy human hunger at its deepest level. Only Jesus, the bread who has come down from heaven, can satisfy the human hunger for life.

Conclusion

I began this chapter by referring to a norm of Jewish religion, giving alms to the poor. This Jewish practice is reflected in John 12:5-8 and 13:29 and perhaps presupposed in 6:5-8. In exploring these passages, I constantly had to peer behind John's christology to detect our thematic. In 12:5-8 our thematic plays a secondary role to Mary's preparation of Jesus for his glorification. In 13:29 it is eclipsed by the powerful symbol of Jesus' washing of his disciples' feet. In 6:5-8 it is quickly forgotten as the reader is caught up in Jesus' discourse on the bread of life. Yet our thematic is present.

As I did my detective work in pursuit of John's use of the thematic of Jesus and the marginalized, I frequently ran into harmonizing tapes and stereotypes, which informed me that Jesus and his disciples did not have money. Their voice and power were so strong that it was difficult to sing my rallying

cry, Let John Be John! But in the end the cry came forth, and
I noted that the Johannine Jesus and his disciples not only
possessed money, but used that money to care for the
marginalized needy.

I mentioned in passing that a possible life situation or *Sitz
im Leben* for this Johannine accent was John's concern to
demonstrate that Jesus observed this Jewish norm of caring
for the poor while abolishing others, e.g., the Jewish ritual of
purification (2:1-11) and the prohibition of association with
Samaritans (4:4-42). As we hinted at the beginning of this
chapter, the Johannine portrait of a Jesus who cares for the
poor may be related to the Jamnian rabbis' concerted efforts
at helping the poor after the Jewish War. John's community,
in the person of Jesus and his disciples, may have abandoned
many Jewish institutions, but it retains the one norm of giving
alms to the marginalized poor. They will not abandon to
starvation those impoverished by the Jewish War. But more
on the Johannine life situation in chapter eight below.

3

Those Who are Ignorant of the Law

In the previous chapter we commenced our study of "Jesus and the marginalized" by examining four explicit Johannine references to "the poor." We found that Jesus and his disciples were obedient to the Jewish norm of providing monetary assistance to those who were on the economic margins of society. In this chapter we continue our exploration of the theme of "Jesus and the marginalized" by looking at one specific kind of marginalized person, those who are marginalized because they are ignorant of God's law. In studying these religiously marginalized persons, we will deal with one verse of John's Gospel, 7:49: "But this crowd, who do not know the law, are accursed." After situating this verse in its immediate context in John's Gospel, I will investigate the meaning of the technical term, "people of the land" (in Hebrew: *am haaretz*), which lies behind the phrase "this crowd who do not know the law." I will conclude the chapter with some comments about the possible life situation of John.

The Immediate Context for John 7:49

The immediate literary and theological context of 7:49 is set by 7:40-52, wherein John uses "the crowd" with some frequency. After quoting this passage and italicizing its occurrences of "the crowd," I will probe the Johannine meaning of "the crowd."

[40]When they heard these words, some of *the crowd* said, 'This is really the prophet.' [41]Others said, 'This is the Christ.' But some said, 'Is the Christ to come from Galilee? 'Has not the scripture said that the Christ is descended from David, and comes from Bethlehem, the village where David was? [43]So there was a division among *the crowd* over him. [44]Some of them wanted to arrest him, but no one laid hands on him. [45]The officers then went back to the chief priests and Pharisees, who said to them, 'Why did you not bring him?' [46]The officers answered, 'No man ever spoke like this man.' [47]The Pharisees answered them, 'Are you led astray, you also? [48]Have any of the authorities or of the Pharisees believed in him? [49]But *this crowd*, who do not know the law, are accursed.' [50]Nicodemus, who had gone to him before, and who was one of them, said to them, [51]'Does our law judge a man without first giving him a hearing and learning what he does?' [52]They replied, 'Are you from Galilee too? Search and you will see that no prophet is to rise from Galilee.'

Culpepper (1983: 131-132) has devoted a brief study to John's use of "the crowd" (*ho ochlos*). He concludes his study of the twenty occurrences of "the crowd" in this way: "John's treatment of the crowd lacks the hostility of his characterization of the Jews. The crowd represents the struggle of those who are open to believing, but neither the scriptures nor the signs lead them to authentic faith. They are the world God loves (3:16)." Culpepper is indeed correct in putting his finger on the "struggle" dimension of the crowd's response to Jesus, especially as seen in John 7. But I would go beyond Culpepper's analysis and argue that in John "the crowd" not only represents folks who are open and struggling to believe in Jesus, but also folks who are held in low esteem and marginalized by the religious leaders. In effect, the religious leaders are saying two things. To the crowd they are saying: look at us, who know God's Law. We do not believe in Jesus. About the crowd they are saying: how can you trust what the crowd believes in because they are ignorant of God's revelation in the Law and thus have no basis for judging between what is from God and what is not from God? The curse of Deuteronomy 27:26 is upon them: "'Cursed be he who does not confirm the words of this law by doing them.'" Let me support my argument in greater detail by entering into a somewhat technical discussion of the Hebrew phrase which lies behind "the crowd who do not know the law" (7:49). This discussion will further illustrate my point that in the eyes of the religious leaders "the crowd" is inferior; the religious leaders marginalize "the crowd" because of its ignorance of God's law.

The Technical Term
"The People of the Land" in John 7:49

Almost to a person, commentators on John 7:49 will have a remark similar to this one based on Lindars (1972: 304): there is abundant evidence that the rabbinic scholars felt superior to the common people, whom they regarded as *am haaretz*, people of the land. While helpful, this observation needs to be fleshed out for its implications about the poverty and marginalization of the "people of the land." After examining the three-fold use of "people of the land" in the Old Testament, I will cite and comment on representative passages from rabbinic literature. At the end of this investigation of the "people of the land" we will be in a better position to see to what extent John 7:49 fits into the theme of Jesus and the marginalized in John's Gospel.

Old Testament Passages

Hermann Strack and Paul Billerbeck (1924: 494) rightly distinguish three usages of "people of the land" (Hebrew: *am haaretz*) in the Old Testament. First, this phrase refers to the entire Jewish people. There are many examples of this usage in the prophet Ezekiel, e.g., 22:29: "The people of the land have practiced extortion and committed robbery; they have oppressed the poor and needy, and have extorted from the sojourner without redress"; 46:3: "The people of the land shall worship at the entrance of that gate before the Lord on the sabbaths and on the new moon."

A second usage refers to the large mass of people in distinction to the rulers, e.g., Jeremiah 1:18: "And I, behold, I make you this day a fortified city, an iron pillar, and bronze walls, against the whole land, against the kings of Judah, its princes, its priests, and the people of the land"; 2 Kings 15:5: "And the Lord smote the king, so that he was a leper to the day of his death, and he dwelt in a separate house. And Jotham the king's son was over the household, governing the people of the land." It should be mentioned in passing that the evidence does not bear out the sociological interpretation which Louis Finkelstein (1962: 761) gave to the texts of this second usage: "The *am ha-aretz* mentioned in the last chapters of Kings as a significant and recognized body in the Commonwealth, apparently represented the 'country' in contrast to the 'city.'"

The final usage occurs in the books of Ezra and Nehemiah and refers to the inhabitants of Judea who did not go into exile and were considered half-pagan, e.g., Ezra 6:21: " ... it (the passover lamb) was eaten by the people of Israel who had returned from exile, and also by every one who had joined them and separated himself from the pollutions of the peoples of the land to worship the Lord, the God of Israel"; Nehemiah 10:30: "We will not give our daughters to the peoples of the land or take their daughters for our sons."

In summary, the second and third usages of "people of the land" set the stage for the rabbinic use of the phrase, for in the second there is a distinction between rulers and common people and in the third there is a distinction between those who observe the law and those who do not. In rabbinic parlance the first usage drops out.

Rabbinic Uses of "The People of the Land"

It is notoriously difficult to give exact dates for rabbinic materials and apply them to New Testament times because they are incorporated in texts, e.g., Mishnah and Babylonian Talmud, which were first written down A.D. 200 and later.

Granted this difficulty, we will proceed with methodological rigor and will use primarily the sayings of rabbis who lived around the time of John's Gospel. Thus, although these sayings are contained in writings which date to A.D. 200 or later, there is high probability that they are authentic and are to be dated earlier than A.D. 200. In brief, my argument is that "people of the land" means those who are ignorant of the law.

In the Mishnah tractate Aboth, which contains sayings of the fathers, we have a quotation from Hillel who flourished ca. 20 B.C.: "He (Hillel) used to say: A brutish man dreads not sin, and a 'people of the land' (*am ha-aretz*) cannot be saintly (*hasid*), and the shamefast man cannot learn, and the impatient man cannot teach, and he that engages overmuch in trade cannot become wise; and where there are no men strive to be a man" (2:6; Danby: 1933 modified, for Danby translates *am ha-aretz* by the interpretive "one ignorant of the law"). At first blush the meaning of this saying is not evident. Yet the parallelism it uses revolves around saintliness, ignorance, learning, and teaching. And if we ask learning, teaching, and ignorance about what, and if we ask what leads to holiness, the implied answer is "the law." With this implied answer in mind, we can unravel the saying. "People of the land" are those who are ignorant of the law and therefore incapable of being a saint. Their status is similar to that of the one who is shamefast and therefore cannot learn the law, and of the one who in his impatience cannot teach the law, and of the one who has no leisure to study the law and become wise.

Mishnah Aboth 3:11 contains a saying from Rabbi Dosa ben Harkinas, who flourished ca. 90 A.D.: "Morning sleep and midday wine and children's talk and sitting in the meeting-houses of the 'people of the land' (*amme-haaretz*) put a man out of the world." This saying deals with things which will cause a person to lose touch with the important things in life: late rising from sleep, wine which will cause one to sleep away the afternoon or not use it profitably, the nonsense which occupies children's banter, and attending the synagogues of the "people of the land." It seems to be implied that the "people of the land" will not help one to learn the meaning of the law, which was to be expounded in the synagogue service. It profits one nothing to attend their synagogue services, for they will only share ignorance of the law with you and not that knowledge which gives insight into life in this world.

The Babylonian Talmud contains a tractate called Pesahim. Section 49b of this tractate contains a saying from Rabbi Akiba, who flourished A.D. 110-135: "It was taught, R. Akiba said: 'When I was an *am ha-aretz* I said: I would that I had a scholar (before me), but I would maul him like an ass.' Said his disciples to him, 'Rabbi, say like a dog'. 'The former bites and breaks the bones, while the latter bites but does not break the bones,' he answered them" (Epstein: 1938). This passage shows the great animosity between the "people of the land," i.e., those ignorant of the law, and the scholars at the time of Akiba. It also shows that "people of the land" are those who are not scholars, that is, they are people who are ignorant of the law. While it may be debatable whether that same degree of animosity existed at the time of John's Gospel (ca. A.D. 90-100), this passage provides evidence of the distinction between those who knew the law and those who did not. These latter are called "people of the land."

Our final rabbinic passage stems from Mishnah Horayoth 3:8, which is not ascribed to any rabbi, but lays down a general principle which accords with the sayings of the three rabbis quoted in our previous examples. The latest date for this quotation is the date of the codification of the Mishnah, A.D. 200. The passage goes: "A priest precedes a levite, a levite an Israelite, an Israelite a bastard, a bastard a *Nathin*, a *Nathin* a proselyte, and a proselyte a freed slave. This applies when they all are (otherwise) equal; but if a bastard is learned in the Law and a High Priest is a 'people of the land' (*am haaretz*), the bastard who is learned in the Law precedes the High Priest who is a 'people of the land' (*am haaretz*)." This, perhaps, is the clearest example of what has been implicit in the previous three examples: "people of the land" means one who does not know the law. It should also be noted that according to this passage one who was "people of the land," that is, ignorant of the law, is not necessarily a peasant or poor. For the high priest, who would be an aristocrat and well-to-do, is called "people of the land" (*am haaretz*), one who does not know the law.

Conclusions to Be Drawn from the Rabbinic Materials for Interpreting John 7:49

From the four rabbinic sayings quoted above it seems clear that behind John 7:49 is the rabbinic term of abuse and marginalization, those who are ignorant of the law/ "people of the land," who are considered inferior by the teachers of the law. Thus, the "crowd" in John 7:40-52, especially 7:49, is not only to be seen as those struggling to believe in Jesus, but also as those who are held in low esteem and marginalized by the religious leaders.

A second conclusion arises from Mishnah Horayoth 3:8 where it is clear that one cannot simply equate those ignorant of the law/"people of the land" with "the poor." This view is seconded by Aharon Oppenheimer (1977: 20), who concludes from his study of "the people of the land":

> Nor is there any justification for regarding the am haaretz as necessarily belonging to a lower or 'plebian' class. The majority of the ammei ha-aretz probably did belong to the masses, but there was no reason why some of them should not have been wealthy and members of the aristocratic and upper classes.

Oppenheimer's evaluation of the rabbinic evidence is confirmed by Ephraim E. Urbach (1975: 632) and Seán Freyne (1980: 308). The point made by these three scholars is well taken. But might I be permitted to accentuate one part of my quotation from Oppenheimer? He wrote: "The majority of the ammei ha-aretz *probably* did belong to the masses." Thus, there is good reason to suppose that the majority of the people referred to in John 7:49 as "ignorant of the law"/"people of the land" were poor. I conclude that John 7:49 should be included under John's theme of Jesus and the marginalized, not only because it refers to a group of people who are marginalized because of their ignorance of the law, but also because the majority of these people are poor.

Our final conclusion has to do with the Synoptic tapes which play in our minds when we hear a passage like John

7:49. From Matt 11:19 and Luke 7:34 we are accustomed to hear the tape playing of how tax collectors and sinners welcomed Jesus whereas the religious leaders did not. But John is John and does not people his Gospel with tax collectors and sinners. He must be heard in his own right as an evangelist who contrasts the ignorant crowd with the learned religious leaders. Put another way, John plays the Synoptic theme of Jesus' association with outcasts in the chord of who knows the Law and how Jesus surpasses the Law. And what is found here in one verse, John 7:49, will be played out in narrative form in John 9 where the man born blind, one of those who are ignorant of the law/"people of the land," sees who Jesus truly is whereas the religious leaders, who know the law, refuse to see Jesus. To anticipate our next chapter's treatment of John 9 a bit: "Jn thus illustrates how *supposed* ignorance of the Law (Jn 7:49; 9:34) leads to Jesus and how *presumed* knowledge of the Law militates against the acknowledgement of Jesus (Jn 7:48; 9:34, 40f; 3:10)" (Pancaro 1955: 288-289). This view of Jesus and the marginalized, of course, is not the Synoptic picture of Jesus and the poor, but nevertheless it is worthy of our consideration. Let John Be John!

The Johannine Sitz Im Leben

The polemic contained in 7:40-52, especially in 7:49, would seem to fit into the common view of the *Sitz im Leben* of John's Gospel, namely, a situation in which the Johannine Jewish Christians were experiencing opposition from the Jewish synagogue because of their christology and lax membership standards (see Martyn 1979). And this polemic is datable to the last years of the first Christian century (Freyne 1980: 307). In this situation John 7:49 would indicate the origin of some of the members of John's community. Those ignorant of the law, many of whom were poor, have been open to and have believed in the Jesus preached by John's community and have joined that community.

The polemic of 7:40-52 also reveals John's negative view of the religious leaders of his time. For it is with great irony that

John, through the person of Nicodemus, depicts how the religious leaders, who glory in their knowledge of the law, do not observe that very law in trying to condemn Jesus: "'Does our law judge a man without first giving him a hearing and learning what he does?'" (7:50). Behind these religious leaders stand the opponents of the Johannine Jewish Christians.

I turn over the podium to Rudolf Bultmann who will recapitulate what we have said in this chapter by refocusing it through the lens of the reversal theme which streams through John 7:40-52:

> Yet the crowd (*ochlos*) is made uneasy by Jesus' words, and in the crowd (*ochlos*) there are believers—however much they may waver—whereas the official authorities, on the whole, remain unshaken; this but serves to illustrate that it is among those who, according to the world's standards, are the most questionable, that we may in the first place expect to find a readiness to receive the word of the Revealer.

4

The Physically Afflicted

In our pursuit of John's theme of Jesus and the marginalized we have already seen how Jesus and his disciples cared for the economically marginalized by giving them alms. We have also seen how those marginalized by the religious leaders because of their ignorance of the law responded openly to Jesus. In this chapter our study moves forward by looking at those marginalized because of physical afflictions. After giving evidence from antiquity for the marginalization of the physically incapacitated, I will explore the terminology John uses to describe the ill. This exploration, in turn, will lead us to a consideration of two Johannine signs: 9:1-41 and 5:1-15. Observations about a possible life situation for this aspect of the larger Johannine theme of Jesus and the marginalized will conclude this chapter.

The Physically Ill Are Marginalized

In this section, in which we restrict ourselves to evidence from the Old Testament and Qumran, we are obviously not talking about those who have colds and flu, but those whose illnesses are chronic or whose afflictions are incapacitating.

It is especially clear in the Old Testament lament psalms that poverty and physical affliction and incapacity went hand in hand, e.g., Psalm 31:10: "My strength is diminished (Greek: *esthenēsen*) in my poverty (Greek: *ptōcheia*), and my bones waste away." As G. Johannes Botterwick (1977: 36) writes of the lament psalms: "The destitution of the poor (*'ebhyon*) is to be inferred from the whole tenor of the appropriate psalms: it manifests itself in affliction, illness, loneliness, and nearness to death..." Job 29:12-17 gives very rich poetic expression, through parallelism of lines, to the equation of the poor with the physically sick:

> [12]Because I delivered the poor (Hebrew: 'ani; Greek: ptō-chon) who cried, and the fatherless who had no one to help him. [13]The blessing of him who was about to perish came upon me, and I caused the widow's heart to sing for joy. [14]I put on righteousness, and it clothed me; my justice was like a robe and a turban. [15]I was eyes to the blind, and feet to the lame. [16]I was a father to the poor (Hebrew: *'ebhyonim*; Greek: *adynaton*), and I searched out the cause of him whom I did not know. [17]I broke the fangs of the unrighteous, and made him drop his prey from his teeth.

Often, in antiquity and in contemporary life, the chronically ill are put on the margins of society and religion by those who are healthy and who control access to the centers of society or of worship. For example, Leviticus 21:17-23 restricts those who can offer worship. It lists the following sons of Aaron as forbidden to offer the bread of God: blind, lame, mutilated face, limb too long, injured foot, injured hand, hunchback, dwarf, defect in sight, itching disease, scabs, crushed testicles, any blemish whatsoever. The covenanters at Qumran, near the Dead Sea, enumerated the following as excluded from participating with them at the messianic banquet: afflicted in flesh, crushed in feet or hands, lame, blind, dumb, defective eyesight, senility (1 QSA ii 5-22). It should be noted that among the marginalized mentioned in Leviticus and at Qumran would be the Johannine characters of 9:1-41 and 5:1-15: the first one has been blind from birth, incapacitated, and reduced to begging whereas the second one does not have the wherewithal to hire someone to put him into the pool's healing waters to find a cure for the illness which has incapacitated him for thirty-eight years.

From the data I have just provided from the Old Testament

and Qumran, which I take to be illustrative of a prevalent attitude, I conclude that incapacitated people were very often poor and were on the fringes of society and religion.

Johannine Terminology for Jesus' Care of the Physically Ill

In our quest to let John be John, let us give brief attention to the way John describes the physically ill. John does not use many words which the Synoptics use to describe illness. He does not refer to sickness by the Greek word *nosos*, which is found ten times in the Synoptics. Nor does he employ for "sickness" the Greek phrase, *kakōs echontes*, which occurs eleven times in the Synoptics. Absent from John is reference to illness as caused by unclean spirits. Only once, in 5:10, does John use the Greek word, *therapeuein*, for "to heal," a word which occurs thirty-one times in the Synoptics. The Synoptics use the Greek adjective, *hygiēs*, for "healthy" three times and the Greek verb, *hygiainein*, for "to be healthy" three times. John uses the adjective "healthy" six times, all in reference to the man who had been ill for thirty-eight years (5:6, 9, 11, 14, 15; 7:23).

But John's favorite word for "sickness" comes from a Greek word, which has the basic meaning of physical weakness (see G. Stählin 1964: 490-493). He uses the noun "sickness" (*astheneia*) twice in 5:5 and 11:4. The verb "to be sick" (*asthenein*) he employs nine times: 4:46; 5:3, 7, 13; 6:2; 11:1, 2, 3, 6. The noun is found in all three Synoptics a total of five times, the verb six times.

It is intriguing to note that at least four times in the Old Testament "poor" is translated by the adjective form (*asthenēs*) of the noun and verb John uses:

> Proverbs 21:13: "He who closes his ear to the cry of the poor (Greek: *asthenous*; Hebrew: *dal*) will himself cry out and not be heard."
> Proverbs 22:22: "Do not rob the poor (Greek: *penēta*; Hebrew: *dal*), because he is poor (Greek: *ptōchos*; Hebrew:

dal) or crush the afflicted (Greek: *asthenē*; Hebrew: *'ani*) at the gate."

Proverbs 31:5: "lest they drink and forget what has been decreed, and pervert the rights of all the afflicted" (Greek: *astheneis*; Hebrew: *bene-'ani*).

Proverbs 31:9: "Open your mouth, judge righteously, maintain the rights of the poor (Greek: *penēta*; Hebrew: *'ani*) and needy" (Greek: *asthenē*; Hebrew: *'ebhyon*).

This Old Testament usage sheds some light on our theme of Jesus and the marginalized. For although John is more concerned theologically with the faith responses the physically weak person gives to Jesus, he still does not totally neglect the fact that Jesus came to give new life to the physically weak, the incapacitated, who are poor.

One final point. Unlike Mark, who has seventeen miracle stories, John has a mere seven (2:1-11; 4:46-54; 5:1-15; 6:1-15; 6:16-21; 9:1-41; 11:1-44), which he calls "signs." While relatively few in number, these signs fit into John's theology of Jesus as the giver of life, whose seventh and therefore perfect sign is raising a person from the dead (11:1-44). By means of his technique of "refrain" John will recall these few signs, e.g., during polemic, and thus create the impression that Jesus has worked more signs than he has. See how John 6:2 refers back to the signs of 4:46-54 and 5:1-15, how 7:21-24 refers back to the sign of 5:1-15, how 10:9, 21; 11:37 refer back to the sign of 9:1-41, and finally how 12:1, 9, 17 refer back to the sign of 11:1-44. This "refrain" technique also invites the reader to ponder the deeper meaning of these signs, e.g., to reflect anew in 10:9, 21 and 11:37 on the significance of Jesus' gifting the blind man with sight, and be led to a stronger faith in Jesus, the Christ and Son of God, in whom one finds life (see 20:30-31). In chapter eight below we will return to these seven signs and view them as God's works effected by Jesus, works which Jesus' disciples are to continue (see 14:12).

Now that our eyes have become adjusted to John's vocabulary for the physically disabled, we will look at two representative and intimately related passages: 9:1-41 and 5:1-15.

JOHN 9:1-41
THE BLIND BEGGAR

9   As he passed by, he saw a man blind from his birth. [2]And his disciples asked him, "Rabbi, who sinned, this man or his parents, that he was born blind?" [3]Jesus answered, "It was not that this man sinned, or his parents, but that the works of God might be made manifest in him. [4]We must work the works of him who sent me, while it is day; night comes, when no one can work. [5]As long as I am in the world, I am the light of the world." [6]As he said this, he spat on the ground and made clay of the spittle and anointed the man's eyes with the clay, [7]saying to him, "Go, wash in the pool of Silóam" (which means Sent). So he went and washed and came back seeing. [8]The neighbors and those who had seen him before as a beggar, said, "Is not this the man who used to sit and beg?" [9]Some said, "It is he"; others said, "No but he is like him." He said, "I am the man." [10]They said to him, "Then how were your eyes opened?" [11]He answered, "The man called Jesus made clay and anointed my eyes and said to me, "Go to Silóam and wash'; so I went and washed and received my sight." [12]They said to him, "Where is he?" He said, "I do not know."

[13]They brought to the Pharisees the man who had former- ly been blind. [14]Now it was a sabbath day when Jesus made the clay and opened his eyes. [15]The Pharisees again asked him how he had received his sight. And he said to them, "He put clay on my eyes, and I washed, and I see." [16]Some of the Pharisees said, "This man is not from God, for he does not keep the sabbath." But others said, "How can a man who is a sinner do such signs?" There was a division among them. [17]So they again said to the blind man, "What do you say about him, since he has opened your eyes?" He said, "He is a prophet." [18]The Jews did not believe that he had been blind and had received his sight, until they called the parents of the man who had received his sight, [19]and asked them, "Is this your son, who you say was born blind? How then does he now see?" [20]His parents answered, "We know that this is our son, and that he was born blind; [21]but

how he now sees we do not know, nor do we know who opened his eyes. Ask him; he is of age, he will speak for himself." ²²His parents said this because they feared the Jews, for the Jews had already agreed that if any one should confess him to be Christ, he was to be put out of the synagogue. ²³Therefore his parents said, "He is of age, ask him." ²⁴So for the second time they called the man who had been blind, and said to him, "Give God the praise; we know that this man is a sinner." ²⁵He answered, "Whether he is a sinner, I do not know; one thing I know, that though I was blind, now I see." ²⁶They said to him, "What did he do to you? How did he open your eyes?" ²⁷He answered them, "I have told you already, and you would not listen. Why do you want to hear it again? Do you too want to become his disciples?" ²⁸And they reviled him, saying, "You are his disciple, but we are disciples of Moses. ²⁹We know that God has spoken to Moses, but as for this man, we do not know where he comes from." ³⁰ The man answered, "Why, this is a marvel! You do not know where he comes from, and yet he opened my eyes. ³¹We know that God does not listen to sinners, but if any one is a worshiper of God and does his will, God listens to him. ³²Never since the world began has it been heard that any one opened the eyes of a man born blind. ³³If this man were not from God, he could do nothing." ³⁴They answered him, "You were born in utter sin, and would you teach us?" And they cast him out. ³⁵Jesus heard that they had cast him out, and having found him he said, "Do you believe in the Son of man?" ³⁶He answered, "And who is he, sir, that I may believe in him?" ³⁷Jesus said to him, "You have seen him, and it is he who speaks to you." ³⁸He said, "Lord, I believe"; and he worshiped him. ³⁹Jesus said, "For judgment I came into this world, that those who do not see may see, and that those who see may become blind." ⁴⁰Some of the Pharisees near him heard this, and they said to him, "Are we also blind?" ⁴¹Jesus said to them, "If you were blind, you would have no guilt; but now that you say, 'We see,' your guilt remains."

After general remarks about the vocabulary and irony of

this story, I will examine three verses in some detail: 9:8; 9:34; 9:39.

As readers would expect in a story which deals with giving sight to a blind person, the Johannine vocabulary for "illness" in general (*astheneia/asthenein*) gives way to more specific vocabulary, especially that of "to open eyes" (9:10, 14, 17, 21, 26, 30, 32; see also 10:21; 11:37). The physical weakness of the man is blindness from birth.

In the profound irony of 9:1-41 the blind beggar, who is ignorant of the law, has his eyes opened ever more deeply into the meaning of Jesus while those who are learned in the law become more and more blind to the meaning of Jesus. Note the progress in the blind beggar's evaluation of Jesus: "the man called Jesus" (9:11); "He is a prophet" (9:17); "If this man were not from God, he could do nothing" (9:33); "Lord, I believe" (9:38). Note the regression in the evaluation of Jesus made by those learned in the law: Jesus may be a sinner or be from God (9:16); "we know that this man is a sinner" (9:24); "we know that God has spoken to Moses, but as for this man, we do not know where he comes from" (9:29). For further details on the irony of John 9:1-41, see Paul D. Duke (1985: 117-126).

While the commentators provide detailed and valuable observations about the vocabulary of "seeing" and the irony of 9:1-41, they give little attention to 9:8 and the fact that the man born blind was a beggar. Bultmann (1971: 333 n. 7) is typical: "The fact that it is only now mentioned that the blind man was a beggar ... is probably to be explained by the narrator's tacit assumption that all blind men were beggars." But this fact is vital for John's theme of Jesus and the marginalized. It is a poor man who has courageously grown in faith, become a disciple of Jesus, and been cast out of the synagogue by the religious leaders.

Further dimensions of the status of the poor man of 9:1-41 are to be seen in 9:34 and 9:39. In Chapter 3 we made allusion to the fact that John 9:1-41 gives narrative expression to John 7:49, that is, the blind beggar is representative of the many poor and marginalized, "the crowd who does not know the law." It is no wonder that the religious leaders will not accept his teaching and cast him out of their synagogue (9:34). Pancaro (1975: 101) has spelled out in a convincing way the fourfold relationship between the story of 9:1-41, especially 9:24-34, and the statements of 7:45-49.

First, the main characters are the same. In 9:24-34 we find the Pharisees, who claim to be disciples of Moses and the beggar born blind, who belongs to the "people of the land," who is born in sin. In 7:45-49 we have the leaders and the Pharisees who are learned in the law; we also have the crowd which ignores the law, with whom the officers are associated.

Second, the religious leaders glory in their knowledge of the law. In 9:24-34 the Pharisees take pride in being disciples of Moses. In 7:45-49 they vaunt their knowledge of the law.

Third, the religious leaders find security in the law and not in Jesus. In 9:24-34 because the religious leaders are faithful disciples of Moses, to whom God spoke, they cannot accept Jesus and his teaching. In 7:45-49 it is their knowledge of the law which has prevented them from accepting Jesus' teaching.

Finally, the religious leaders are superior to those who are ignorant of the law. In 9:24-34 the Pharisees treat the beggar as an inferior and marginalize him. He belongs to the "people of the land," is born in sin, and should not presume to teach them. In 7:45-49 they revile the officers and curse the crowd, which is ignorant of the law. If the blind man has become a disciple of Jesus, it is because he belongs to the "people of the land." The crowd has believed in Jesus because they, too, are ignorant of the law.

In sum, this beggar is one of "the people of the land," ignorant of the law. Although judged to be an inferior and cast out of the synagogue (9:34), this poor man is superior to the religious leaders. For he grows in faith in Jesus and finally confesses Jesus as Lord.

John 9:39 is of a piece with 9:8 and 9:34, for it describes the beggar as "one who does not see." If one uses the criterion that being learned in the law is equivalent to seeing, then it is true that the beggar does not see and is consequently an inferior, a marginal one, a person who belongs to the "people of the land." But in his ironic presentation the evangelist thinks differently of the beggar, who was born blind, and now sees and believes in the light which is Jesus. For John the blind man is a hero.

In conclusion, John 9:1-41 shows how Jesus has had mercy on a man who has been physically incapacitated since birth and thus marginalized from society and a beggar. This marginalized person, instead of being accepted back into society after he has received his sight, is interrogated by the religious leaders. Under interrogation he grows in faith in Jesus and is finally thrown out of the synagogue by the religious leaders for trying to teach them the meaning of God's law. How dare an ignoramus in the law teach the teachers! As the man, born blind, but now seeing, wanders about as an outcast from the synagogue, he again meets Jesus who welcomes him into his communion.

JOHN 5:1-15
A POOR MAN WHO DOES NOT COME
TO FAITH IN JESUS

5   After this there was a feast of the Jews, and Jesus went up to Jerusalem.
²Now there is in Jerusalem by the Sheep Gate a pool, in Hebrew called Bethza'tha, which has five porticoes. ³In these lay a multitude of invalids, blind, lame, paralyzed. ⁵One man was there, who had been ill for thirty-eight years. ⁶When Jesus saw him and knew that he had been lying there a long time, he said to him, "Do you want to be healed?" ⁷The sick man answered him, "Sir, I have no man to put me into the pool when the water is troubled, and while I am going another steps down before me." ⁸Jesus said to him, "Rise, take up your pallet, and walk." ⁹And at once the man was healed, and he took up his pallet and walked.
Now that day was the sabbath. ¹⁰So the Jews said to the man who was cured, "It is the sabbath, it is not lawful for you to carry your pallet." ¹¹But he answered them, "The man who healed me said to me, 'Take up your pallet, and walk.'" ¹²They asked him, "Who is the man who said to you, 'Take up your pallet, and walk'?" ¹³Now the man who

had been healed did not know who it was, for Jesus had withdrawn, as there was a crowd in the place. [14]Afterward, Jesus found him in the temple, and said to him, "See, you are well! Sin no more, that nothing worse befall you." [15]The man went away and told the Jews that it was Jesus who had healed him.

As we will see, this passage is closely related to 9:1-41. But before delving into this relationship, we should attend to matters of vocabulary and such like. In all this we will be guided by the insight of Edwyn C. Hoskyn (1940: 265), who commented on our passage: "The Evangelist records a signal act of charity towards a poor man." The favorite Johannine vocabulary for "sick" as physically weak (*astheneia/asthenein*) occurs in 5:3, 5, 7, 13. And as we noted earlier in this chapter, this usage may be the Johannine way of saying that the lame man was poor. Furthermore, the man is incapacitated and has been so for thirty-eight years; he lives on the margins of society.

Besides the passage's vocabulary a key to interpreting 5:1-15 is to be found in the parallels between John 5:1-15 and 9:1-41, which are so extensive that it seems that the evangelist intended his readers to compare and contrast the two marginalized characters involved. I adapt my list of parallels from that of Culpepper (1983: 139-140):

The Lame Man	*The Blind Beggar*
1) The man's history is described (38 years; 5:5)	1) The man's history is described (from birth; 9:1)
2) Jesus takes the initiative to heal (5:6)	2) Jesus takes the initiative to heal (9:6)
3) The pool (Bethesda) has healing powers for some	3) The man washes in the pool (Siloam) and is healed (9:7)
4) The sick person has no man to put him into the pool (5:7)	4) The blind man is a beggar (9:8)
5) Jesus heals on the sabbath (5:9)	5) Jesus heals on the sabbath (9:14)

6) The Jews accuse him of violating the sabbath (5:10)

6) The Pharisees charge that Jesus violated the sabbath (9:16)

7) The Jews ask who healed him (5:12)

7) The Pharisees ask how he was healed (9:15)

8) The man does not know where Jesus is or who he is (5:13)

8) The man does not know where Jesus is (9:12)

9) Jesus finds him (5:14) and invites belief

9) Jesus finds him (9:35) and invites belief

10) The man goes to the Jews (5:15)

10) The Jews cast the man out (9:34-35)

What is one to make of these extensive similarities? It seems that John has set up the extensive parallels between 9:1-41 and 5:1-15, especially in #7-10, to contrast two marginal persons. The blind beggar deepens his appreciation of this liberation and stands up for Jesus against the religious leaders. The man, who had been sick for almost a lifetime and has been restored to wholeness by Jesus, does not stand up for Jesus, but rather joins forces with the religious leaders against his liberator and betrays Jesus (see Whitacre 1982: 115-116).

We conclude from the purposeful parallels between 5:1-15 and 9:1-41 that John is no romantic. In his realism he realizes that marginalized persons, who are liberated by Jesus from incapaciting illness, are not necessarily going to embark on the arduous journey of faith. Two marginalized persons are cured by Jesus. A poor blind beggar is open to receive Jesus. A man, who has been lame for thirty-eight years, does not receive Jesus.

Reflections on a Possible Johannine Life Situation

As Brown (1979) and Martyn (1979) have argued, the Johannine life situation has as one of its major components hostility between the Johannine community and the Jewish synagogue. That *Sitz im Leben* fits 9:1-41 quite well, for the man born blind, the hero of Johannine Christians, is thrown out of the Jewish synagogue because he believes in Jesus. Members of John's community, enlightened by the light of Jesus, will be persecuted and are to be as strong in their faith under interrogation as the man born blind. They are encouraged, because even if they are cast out of the synagogue (9:34), Jesus will never cast them out of his sight (see 6:37).

A life situation of persecution also fits the story of 5:1-15. As Martyn (1979: 71) writes:

> *The lame man* ... represents the Jew who, though presumably thankful to be healed, nevertheless remains wholly loyal to the synagogue. When members of the Gerousia ask him to identify his healer (5:12) and thus to participate, albeit passively, in whatever hostile steps they may take against the healer, he complies with their request.

In their proclamation and sharing of Jesus' healing power with synagogue members the Johannine Christians will meet with betrayal and persecution as seen in what happened to Jesus in 5:1-47. But that should not discourage them in their mission. As the parallels between 5:1-15 and 9:1-41 indicate, all mission is not failure. They can always be buoyed up by the "success" story of 9:1-41.

In conclusion, this chapter has contributed additional building blocks to our thesis that John does develop a theme of Jesus and the marginalized. But again, as we have seen earlier, he does it in his own way. The physically afflicted poor do occur in his Gospel, but are not highlighted, as is frequently the case in the Synoptic Gospels, as objects of Jesus' mercy. John presents them from the perspective of how they respond to Jesus in faith. Indeed, this way of going about evangelical matters is not that of the Synoptics. But let John Be John!

5

Geographically Marginalized People: The Royal Official and the Samaritans

In previous chapters we considered individuals who were marginalized because of poverty, ignorance of the law, or incapacitating illness. In this chapter we single out those who are marginalized because of their place of origin: the Judeans look down upon the royal official who is a Galilean; Jews deem people from Samaria inferior. Of course, in each instance there is also a religious basis for marginalization, for both Galileans and Samaritans are ignorant of the law. But the key reason for marginalization is geographical origin.

This type of marginalization is not unfamiliar to us. In the United States there are Yankees and southerners; city slickers and country hicks. In Chicago there are southsiders and northsiders. In the St. Louis area there are city dwellers and county dwellers. There is northern Ireland and the rest of Ireland. The list could be extended almost indefinitely. But my point is made: we have a base in our own experience for appreciating what John is talking about in chapter 4 of his Gospel.

In this chapter I will first set the two stories of John 4 in literary and scholarly contexts. Then after examining each one in turn for its contributions to John's theme of Jesus and the marginalized, I will conclude with some observations about John's possible life situation.

Literary and Scholarly Context of John 4

John's stories of the royal official (4:46-54) and the Samaritans (4:4-42) conclude a sequence of stories which, beginning with 2:1, deal with the way individuals have responded to Jesus. There is scholarly consensus that such a sequence exists on a literary level. Scholars, however, are not in agreement about whether there is a more developed theological pattern in this sequence.

Francis J. Moloney (1978: 201) is representative of those scholars who have found a highly developed pattern in 2:1-4:54. The pattern opens in 2:1-11 with a story of Jesus' Mother's complete faith in him in a Jewish context. This opening frame is followed by the examples of individuals who show different levels of faith in Jesus in a Jewish and non-Jewish context respectively: the Jews of 2:12-22 and the Samaritan woman (4:1-15) have *no faith*; the Jewish leader, Nicodemus (3:1-21) and the Samaritan woman (4:16-26) have *partial faith;* John the Baptist (3:22-36) and the Samaritan villagers (4:27-30, 39-42) have *complete faith.* Thus, in the Jewish context we see the sequence of the no faith of the Jerusalem Jews, the partial faith of Nicodemus, and the complete faith of John the Baptist. In the non-Jewish context we have the no faith of the Samaritan woman followed by her partial faith which in turn is followed by the complete faith of her fellow Samaritan villagers. John concludes the pattern in 4:43-54 with the frame of the story of complete faith in Jesus in a non-Jewish context. Moloney (1978: 196) sees the rationale for this pattern in this way: "It must be stressed at this stage that the whole 'progression' from one state to another is not a condemnation or canonization of any group or person. The examples are used as a model of various types of faith, *all of which* could be the experience of the reader." At this stage of our investigation it is imperative to note that Moloney (1978: 211 n. 45) interprets 4:43-54 as an example of the complete faith of a non-Jew or pagan: "The least one can conclude is that there is every possibility that the *basilikos* (royal official) was a non-Jew."

Other scholars are not persuaded that any developed theological pattern exists in the sequence of stories from 2:1-4:54.

Raymond E. Brown (1966: cxliii-cxliv), for example, groups the stories together under the general rubric of "different reactions of individuals and groups to Jesus." He continues:

> "The temptation is to find a logical development in this sequence. One that has been suggested is a growth of faith from Nicodemus, a Jew, through the Samaritan woman (a half-Jew) to the royal official, a Gentile. However, the designation of the official as a Gentile is on the basis of his identification with the Synoptic centurion; John does not mention it, and the evangelist can scarcely have expected the readers to guess it."

It is important to note that Brown does not think there is sufficient evidence to justify the conclusion that the royal official of 4:46-54 is a Gentile.

For our purposes two points may be drawn from this scholarly discussion of the context of 4:4-54: 1) there is a consensus that the Samaritans were outside the boundaries of God's people; in our terms, they were geographically marginalized; 2) there is much dispute over whether the royal official of 4:46-54 is a Gentile and therefore outside the pale of God's people, that is, one who is marginalized.

In what follows I will begin with John 4:43-54, for, if the royal official is not a Gentile, serious doubt might be cast on the validity of my thesis that John develops the theme of Jesus and the marginalized. It must be treated first and not relegated to the end of this chapter when my readers may be fatigued. I also treat it first because my discussion of 4:4-42 at the end of this chapter will easily lead into the material of my next chapter, The Women in John's Gospel. In advance, I tell my readers that it is my contention that John 4:43-54 does deal with someone who is marginalized, but not because he is a Gentile, but because he is a Galilean. As such, he is representative of those who are geographically marginalized.

JOHN 4:43-54
A DESPISED GALILEAN BELIEVES IN JESUS' WORD

43After the two days he departed to Galilee. 44For Jesus himself testified that a prophet has no honor in his own country. 45So when he came to Galilee, the Galileans welcomed him, having seen all that he had done in Jerusalem at the feast, for they too had gone to the feast.

46So he came again to Cāna in Galilee, where he had made the water wine. And at Capernaum there was an official whose son was ill. 47When he heard that Jesus had come from Jüdēa to Galilee, he went and begged him to come down and heal his son, for he was at the point of death. 48Jesus therefore said to him, "Unless you see signs and wonders you will not believe." 49The official said to him, "Sir, come down before my child dies." 50Jesus said to him, "Go; your son will live." The man believed the word that Jesus spoke to him and went his way. 51As he was going down, his servants met him and told him that his son was living. 52So he asked them the hour when be began to mend, and they said to him, "Yesterday at the seventh hour the fever left him." 53The father knew that was the hour when Jesus had said to him, "Your son will live"; and he himself believed, and all his household. 54This was now the second sign that Jesus did when he had come from Jü·dē' a to Galilee.

The Royal Official is not a Gentile

In chapter one above we cautioned against our common tendency to harmonize the various gospel accounts of one incident and to form one composite account. In chapter two above we noticed that harmonizing-itis might prevent us from appreciating the uniqueness of John 6:5-8. The danger of harmonizing is perhaps strongest in the instance at hand, for most of us are bent on reading John 4:46-54 through the eyes of Luke 7:1-10 and Matt 8:5-13. In both of these Synoptic stories the man, whose faith is praised, is a centurion at Capernaum. And the stories themselves make it absolutely clear that this centurion is not a Jew, but a Gentile. If we read John 4:46-54

very carefully, we will note that the man is not called a centurion, nor is there any clear indication in the text that he is a
Gentile. One will look in vain for something similar to Luke
7:5: "for he loves our nation, and he built us our synagogue";
or Matt 8:10: "Truly, I say to you, not even in Israel have I
found such faith."

Now that we are aware of the tape which plays a harmonized
version of this account before our mind's eye, let's take a look
at 4:46-54 in more detail. The hero of this story comes from
Capernaum (4:46), which along with all the rest of Galilee, was
ruled by Herod Antipas during Jesus' ministry. Although his
official title was tetrarch, Herod Antipas was popularly known
as a king. See the story of his birthday party in Matt 14:1-12,
which begins by calling Herod a tetrarch (14:1) and then in
mid-story (14:9) refers to him as a "king." A second point deals
with 4:48, whose significance for our study of the meaning of
basilikos, is well captured by Bultmann (1971: 206 n. 7): "Also
Jesus' reply in v. 48 in John can have been addressed only to a
Jew." Whatever philological data we bring to bear on the
meaning of *basilikos* in 4:46 (4:49), we must remember that
the Johannine context of 4:48 indicates that this "royal person"
was a Jew, specifically a Galilean. Finally, there is 4:46 to
which we will devote considerable space. In 4:46, which also
contains the favorite Johannine word for "being sick" (*esthe-
nei*), the hero is called *basilikos* (see also 4:49). And as we saw
earlier in this chapter, the meaning of this Greek word is
disputed. The dispute centers around two questions: Is the
basilikos a soldier? Is he a Gentile? In our discussion of the
meaning of *basilikos* we will keep these two questions in clear
focus.

Using evidence primarily from Josephus, whose writings
give considerable attention to Herod the Great and his sons
and who was a contemporary of the evangelist, I maintain that
basilikos has two possible meanings in John 4:46 (4:49): 1) a
soldier in the service of the king; 2) a functionary in the service
of the king.

Barrett (1978: 247) summarizes the data from Josephus
which illustrates the first meaning of *basilikos*: "Josephus uses
the word of troops in the service of a king, generally (as at *Bel.*

I, 45), and especially of forces serving the Herods (as at *Vita*, 400f.)." Barrett's first illustration, from Josephus' *Jewish War*, reads: "For, long and stubborn as was the resistance of the Jews, the king's forces (*hoi basilikoi*) with superior numbers and favoured by fortune, were victorious" (Loeb Classical Library Translation). Here the reference is to the troops of King Antiochus. Barrett's second illustration, from Josephus' *Life*, describes the plan of Josephus himself to subdue the troops of King Agrippa: "The next day, after laying an ambuscade in a ravine not far from their earthworks, I offered battle to the royal troops (*tous basilikous*), directing my division to retire until they had lured the enemy forward; as actually happened" (Loeb Classical Library Translation). It should be observed that in these two examples from Josephus it is the context which indicates that *hoi basilikoi* should be interpreted to mean "royal troops." Other instances of *hoi basilikoi* with the meaning of "royal troops" are: *Jewish War* II, 52, 55, 423, 426, 431, 437, 634; III, 69; V, 47, 474; *Jewish Antiquities* XVII, 270, 281, 283; *Life*, 402.

So far we have seen that *basilikos* is used in Josephus in the meaning of "royal soldier." Evidence can be mustered to show that such "royal soldiers" may have been non-Jews. Thus, if one is permitted to think that King Herod the Great's son, Herod Antipas, inherited his father's paranoia of being overthrown by the Jews, then Antipas' "royal troops" (*hoi basilikoi*) would be composed chiefly of non-Jewish mercenaries. See the account of King Herod the Great's funeral in Josephus' *Jewish Antiquities* XVII. 198-199:

> Round the bier were his sons and a host of his relatives, and after them came the army disposed according to the various nationalities and designations. They were arranged in the following order: first came his bodyguards, then the Thracians, and following them, whatever Germans he had, and next came the Gauls. These men were all equipped for battle. Right behind them came the whole army as if marching to war, led by their company-commanders and lower officers, and they were followed by five hundred servants carrying spices (Loeb Classical Library Translation).

So, if Herod Antipas did continue his father's policy of hiring non-Jewish mercenaries, then the *basilikos* of Capernaum may not only have been a soldier, but also a non-Jew. But does the *basilikos* of John 4:46 (4:49), read without the tape of Matt 8:5-13 and Luke 7:1-10 playing in our ears and without Josephus' military context, clearly mean "royal soldier," and a non-Jewish one at that?

And so we are led to explore the second meaning of *basilikos*, that is, "a functionary in the service of the king." The clearest example of *basilikos* with this meaning occurs in Josephus, *Jewish War* II, 595-597:

> About this time some young men of the village of Dabaritha ... laid an ambush for Ptolemy, the overseer of Agrippa and Bernice, and robbed him of all the baggage which he was convoying, including a large number of rich vestments, a quantity of silver goblets and six hundred pieces of gold. Being unable to dispose secretly of such booty, they brought the whole to Josephus, then at Tarichaeae. He censured them for this act of violence to royal officials (*tous basilikous*) (based on Loeb Classical Library Translation).

We should also note that the "royal functionary" described by Josephus was a Jew, for in Josephus' *Life* 128 we learn that Ptolemy was a "compatriot" (*homophylos*) of Josephus. Other examples of *basilikos* with the meaning of "royal functionary" may be found in Josephus' *Jewish War* VII,106; Plutarch, *Solon*, 27; and Polybius, *Histories* IV.76, 2. Some papyri evidence suggests that *basilikos* might even mean "royal secretary," a high ranking official in town government (see Moulton and Milligan 1915: 105).

So we see from this evidence that *basilikos* does not have to mean "soldier" in the service of the king. We see further that a "royal official," who serves a Jewish King, can himself be a Jew. While the *basilikos* of John 4:46 may not have been such a high ranking official as Ptolemy, he, nevertheless, might be a royal official, directly subject to "King" Herod Antipas.

Additional evidence that the *basilikos* means "royal functionary" and not "soldier" may be found in the fact that this individual is employed at Capernaum, which was a border town in Herod Antipas' reign. Through it flowed people and goods from Damascus to the Mediterranean Sea. In it many tolls and import taxes were to be collected; and many and various types of royal administrative officials would be employed there (see Brown 1966: 190). Harold W. Hoehner (1972: 97-100) provides evidence about the "royal officials" present in another Galilean city, Tiberias, whose administrative structure may have been similar in many ways to that of Capernaum.

Let me summarize the complex data I have shared with my readers. First, the *basilikos* is not a royal soldier. It is the Synoptic account of the centurion in Matt 8:5-13 and Luke 7:1-10 that prompts us to interpret the Greek word, *basilikos*, in John 4:46 (and 4:49) as a Gentile soldier. While it is true that *basilikos* can have the meaning of "royal (soldier)" in Josephus, the military context in which it occurs is constitutive of this meaning. The word itself does not carry the meaning of "royal *soldier*." And such a military context is not present in John 4:46-54. Secondly, there is the evidence from Josephus that a "royal functionary" could be a Jew. Further, as we saw above, the Johannine context of 4:48 indicates that the "royal functionary" was a Jew.

In conclusion, the evidence suggests that *basilikos* in John 4:46 (and 4:49) should be paraphrased as a "Jewish royal official, directly subject to 'King' Herod Antipas." The *basilikos* is not a Gentile and therefore a person marginalized from the people of God. John 4:46-54 does not accentuate the faith of a Gentile royal soldier nor is it the culmination of an intricate theological pattern of various types of faith which began in John 2:1.

The Royal Official Is a Galilean

Having shown that the royal official of 4:46-54 is not a marginalized person because he is a Gentile, I want to discuss this passage from a different perspective. This fresh perspective presents the royal official as a Galilean, who is a geographically marginalized person. Here is my case.

Wayne A. Meeks (1966; 1967: 39-41) and Robert T. Fortna (1974) have put us on the trail of seeing the importance of Galilee in 4:46-54. They note that the evangelist is peculiarly redundant in mentioning five times that Galilee is the location of Jesus' second sign. See 4:43: "he departed to Galilee"; 4:45: "So when he came to Galilee, the Galileans welcomed him..."; 4:46: "So he came again to Cana in Galilee..."; 4:47: "When he heard that Jesus had come from Judea to Galilee..."; 4:54: "This was now the second sign that Jesus did when he had come from Judea to Galilee." Further, the evangelist presents the Galileans somewhat positively, for they welcome Jesus (4:45). However, their acceptance of him seems to remain on the level of seeking him for the benefits of his marvelous deeds.

Alerted to the importance the evangelist places in Galilee and the Galileans in our passage, let us return to John 4:48 which I indicated above was a key factor in the interpretation of the meaning of *basilikos* in 4:46 (and 4:49) as a *Jewish* royal official. John 4:48 contains the plural "you" and might be translated: "Unless *you all* see signs and wonders, you all will not believe." To whom does the evangelist refer since he narrates that Jesus is apparently addressing one person only, the "royal official"? In an important article Charles H. Giblin (1980: 204) provides a convincing answer to our question:

> "Jesus' *negative response* (in 4:48) has a twofold scope. As elsewhere, notably in Jesus' reply to Nathanael (1.51), the response directed to an individual looks also beyond him to the group that the addressee helps typify. Here, the royal official (deliberately, perhaps, *not* called a centurion) becomes the focal point for Jesus' words to the other Galileans (who are supposedly Jews, cf. 4.45).

Giblin's explanation of the evangelist's use of the plural "you all" persuades me to take the royal official as typifying the Galileans who seek after the benefits of Jesus' signs (see 4:45). And as the story continues and concludes, we find that this Galilean royal official has model faith, believing not in signs, but solely in Jesus' word (4:50). As Fortna (1974: 86 n. 81) rightly observes: "The nobleman illustrates the exceptional quality of Galilean faith, for he believes *before* he has seen signs and wonders." It seems that for John's community this Galilean is a hero.

In order to appreciate fully what the evangelist is saying in this story, we have to probe more deeply into the meaning he has given to "Galilean." And in doing so, we will touch base again with some of the data we presented in chapter three above on John 7:49. In John 7:41 ("But some said, 'Is the Christ to come from Galilee?'") and John 7:52 ("They replied, 'Are you from Galilee too? Search and you will see that no prophet is to rise from Galilee.'"), we see that "Galilee" is a derogatory word on the lips of the religious leaders from Judea and implies geographical marginalization. No good can be expected to come from Galilee (see 1:46), for Galileans are ignorant of the law and therefore "people of the land" (in Hebrew: *am haaretz*).

Evidence for Galilee as a word of geographical marginalization can be found outside John's Gospel. Seán Freyne (1980: 393) concludes his detailed study of Galilee with these remarks, which are largely based on rabbinic materials:

> As long as the temple survived, 'the other way' of the *halakhah* (oral law and tradition) had little attraction for the country people, and there were few Pharisaic scribes active in the province though occasional attempts to extend their influence to the region can be seen from the ministry of Jesus and the mission of Johanan ben Zakkai. This is understandable since Pharisaism as a way of life was more suited to the middle class townspeople.... After 70 C.E. however, there was a much more concerted effort to win Galilee for the *halakhah*, and partial success at least can be seen in the occurrence of native Galilean rabbis, active both in the province and at Jamnia, as well as in the journeys of the leading Jewish figures to the province. Yet the fact that the *'am ha-'aretz* were still present there after 135 C.E. when rabbinic Judaism was forced to make its home in Galilee, shows that the efforts of the Jamnian period were not altogether successful.

Freyne's summary can be illustrated in the person of Rabbi Johanan ben Zakkai. The frustration which this Judean rabbi experienced after eighteen years spent in Galilee is seen in two facts. During that long period of time he made only one disciple and adjudicated only two cases. It is small wonder that to him is attributed the saying: "O Galilee, Galilee! Thou hatest the Torah!" (Jerusalem Talmud, Shabbat 16.7). Recall the sober experience of missionaries who have labored for twenty years in a foreign land and have made only two "converts."

The Judaean rabbis' frustration with the Galileans' inability to learn is also illumined from the Babylonian Talmud Erubin 53a: "'The Galileans were not exact in their language.' For instance? A certain Galilean once went about inquiring, 'who has *amar*?' 'Foolish Galilean', they said to him, 'do you mean an 'ass' for riding, 'wine' for drinking, 'wool' for clothing or a 'lamb' for killing?" (Epstein 1938). Much of this saying may be lost on us because of the various Hebrew ways of vocalizing and spelling *amar* with their attendant different meanings. But enough of it comes through to us (especially those of us who have made blunders in speaking foreign languages) for us to see the low opinion the Judaean scholars had of the Galileans. In this context, I recall my Spanish experience of congratulating someone on his birthday and instead of saying *año* (year) said *ano* (anus). I was also accustomed to pronouncing *todos* (all) *toros* (bulls) and got myself into trouble when I thought I was telling a group of religious men: "Let us all go." I was heard to exclaim: "Let us bulls go." The Judeans maintained that the Galileans' sloppy language habits prevented them from being seriously concerned with the exact meaning of the words of the law. They were indeed "ignorant of the law," "people of the land," *am haaretz.*

To sum up, our analyses of 4:43-54, especially of 4:45 and 4:48, indicate that the royal official is a Galilean, whose faith in Jesus is exemplary. The evidence from within John's Gospel (7:40, 52) and the evidence just cited from Freyne demonstrate that the Galileans were held in low regard by the Judaean rabbis. If we put this data into the categories of this study, we would conclude that the *basilikos* of 4:46 (and 4:49) is truly a marginal person. He is such not because he is a Gentile, but because he is a Galilean, and as such is despised by the power-ful Judaean rabbis. He is representative of those who are geographically marginalized.

Although the possible Johannine *Sitz im Leben* of John 4 will be explored in depth at the end of this chapter, it would be beneficial to anticipate that discussion somewhat at this point. From John 4:45-54 and other Johannine texts, it seems that John's community reached out to the geographically margina-lized Galileans and depicted them favorably in their Gospel. The comment of Freyne (1980: 379) is well taken: "Perhaps then, John's ironic dismissal of 'this people who does not know the law that is accursed' by the Pharisees (*Jn* 7:49) has a polemical *and* missionising edge to it, as the gospel circulated towards the end of the first century." The Johannine com-munity is intent on preaching its Gospel to certain Galilean Jews and has won some of them over as converts.

JOHN 4:4-42
DESPISED SAMARITANS BELIEVE IN JESUS
AND HIS WORD

[4]He had to pass through Samaria. [5]So he came to a city of Samaria, called Sȳ'chãr, near the field that Jacob gave to his son Joseph. [6]Jacob's well was there, and so Jesus, wearied as he was with his journey, sat down beside the well. It was about the sixth hour.

[7]There came a woman of Samâria to draw water. Jesus said to her, "Give me a drink." [8]For his disciples had gone away into the city to buy food. [9]The Samâritan woman said to him, "How is it that you, a Jew, ask a drink of me, a woman of Samâria?" For Jews have no dealings with Samâritans. [10]Jesus answered her, "If you knew the gift of God, and who it is that is saying to you, 'Give me a drink,' you would have asked him and he would have given you living water." [11]The woman said to him, "Sir, you have nothing to draw with, and the well is deep; where do you get that living water? [12]Are you greater than our father Jacob, who gave us the well, and drank from it himself, and

his sons, and his cattle?" [13]Jesus said to her, "Every one who drinks of this water will thirst again, [14]but whoever drinks of the water that I shall give him will never thirst; the water that I shall give him will become in him a spring of water welling up to eternal life." [15]The woman said to him, "Sir, give me this water, that I may not thirst, nor come here to draw."

[16]Jesus said to her, "Go, call your husband, and come here." [17]The woman answered him, "I have no husband." Jesus said to her, "You are right in saying, 'I have no husband'; [18]for you have had five husbands, and he whom you now have is not your husband; this you said truly." [19]The woman said to him, "Sir, I perceive that you are a prophet. [20]Our fathers worshiped on this mountain;* and you say that in Jerusalem is the place where men ought to worship." [21]Jesus said to her, "Woman, believe me, the hour is coming when neither on this mountain nor in Jerusalem will you worship the Father. [22]You worship what you do not know; we worship what we know, for salvation is from the Jews. [23]But the hour is coming, and now is, when the true worshipers will worship the Father in spirit and truth, for such the Father seeks to worship him. [24]God is spirit, and those who worship him must worship in spirit and truth." [25]The woman said to him, "I know that Messiah is coming (he who is called Christ); when he comes, he will show us all things." [26]Jesus said to her, "I who speak to you am he."

[27]Just then his disciples came. They marveled that he was talking with a woman, but none said, "What do you wish?" or, "Why are you talking with her?" [28]So the woman left her water jar, and went away into the city, and said to the people, [29]"Come, see a man who told me all that I ever did. Can this be the Christ?" [30]They went out of the city and were coming to him.

[31]Meanwhile the disciples besought him, saying, "Rabbi, eat." [32]But he said to them, "I have food to eat of which you do not know." [33]So the disciples said to one another, "Has any one brought him food?" [34]Jesus said to them, "My food is to do the will of him who sent me, and to accomplish his

work. [35]Do you not say, There are yet four months, then comes the harvest'? I tell you, lift up your eyes, and see how the fields are already white for harvest. [36]He who reaps receives wages, and gathers fruit for eternal life, so that sower and reaper may rejoice together. [37]For here the saying holds true, 'One sows and another reaps.' [38]I sent you to reap that for which you did not labor; others have labored, and you have entered into their labor."

[39]Many Samâritans from that city believed in him because of the woman's testimony, "He told me all that I ever did." [40]So when the Samâritans came to him, they asked him to stay with them; and he stayed there two days. [41]And many more believed because of his word. [42]They said to the woman, "It is no longer because of your words that we believe, for we have heard for ourselves, and we know that this is indeed the Savior of the world."

Space limitations will restrict our consideration of this multi-dimensional passage to what it contributes to our theme of Jesus and the marginalized. After giving some details on the animosity between Samaritans and Jews, we will look at select verses.

Samaritans as Geographically Marginalized People

Perhaps, the clearest summary statement about "the Samaritans" is found in Joseph A. Fitzmyer (1981: 829):

'Samaritan' (Greek *Samaritēs*) was originally a geographic term, an inhabitant of Samaria (Hebrew *someron*), the capital of the northern kingdom, founded by Omri ca. 870 B.C. In time it became an ethnic and religious name for the inhabitants of the area between Judea and Galilee, west of the Jordan. The origin of the split of the Samaritans from the Jews is shrouded in mystery and explained differently in each group. . . . In any case, these (half-Jewish?) worshipers of Yahweh . . . built a temple on part of Mount Gerizim

(Tell er-Ras) in Hellenistic times.... From Hellenistic times on the sharp division of Jews and Samaritans is clear; the Samaritans developed their own form of the Pentateuch (redacted in Hasmonean times), their own liturgy (modern Samaritans from Nablus still celebrate the Passover in the open atop Mount Gerizim), and their own liturgical literature in both Hebrew and Aramaic.

The hostility between the Samaritans and the Jews is illustrated by a passage in Josephus' *Jewish Antiquities*, which reports an event which transpired around A.D. 50:

Hatred also arose between the Samaritans and the Jews for the following reason. It was the custom of the Galilaeans at the time of a festival to pass through the Samaritan territory on their way to the Holy City. On one occasion, while they were passing through, certain of the inhabitants of a village called Ginaë, which was situated on the border between Samaria and the Great Plain, joined battle with the Galilaeans and slew a great number of them (XX, 118 in the Loeb Classical Library translation).

The evidence I have presented, although brief, does show that the Samaritans were marginalized by the Jews. Although religious and other factors were surely reasons for their marginalization, they were also marginalized because of geographical origin in the same way that hill-billies, Hoosiers, and Yankees are today. The marginalized status of the Samaritans will become more clear in the study of selected verses which follows.

Study of Selected Verses

Verse nine provides us with a clear example of the strained relationship between Jews and Samaritans, between a Jewish man and a Samaritan woman: "But the Samaritan woman said to him, 'You are a Jew—how can you ask me, a Samari-

tan, for a drink?' (Jews, remember, use nothing in common
with Samaritans)" (translation of Brown 1966: 166). Since the
Samaritans did not observe all the regulations which the Jews
did, there was always the suspicion that they, and especially
their women of menstruation age, would be unclean. And this
uncleanness would be transmitted to the vessel the woman was
carrying, especially if she had drunk from it. And John's story
portrays Jesus as ignoring this ritual barrier and inviting himself to drink from the vessel of a marginalized person.

Verse nine is complemented by verses 39-40 at the end of
the story: "Many Samaritans from that city believed in him
because of the woman's testimony, 'He told me all that I ever
did.' So when the Samaritans came to him, they asked him to
stay with them; and he stayed there two days." The barriers of
hostility between Jew and Samaritan, noted in verse nine,
have fallen away. The Samaritans invite Jesus, a Jewish for-
eigner, to live in their houses. And he accepts quarters among
these outcast and marginalized people. But there is more. The
Greek word *menein* which is translated here as "to stay" also
has a more profound theological sense in John's Gospel and
may be translated as "to dwell." "'To dwell' with Jesus is to
have direct contact with him, to share in his relationship with
God. The note with which v. 40 concludes, therefore, is not
just an incidental narrative detail but an important commentary on Jesus' relationship with the Samaritans" (O'Day 1986:
87). On the level of ironic truth which pulsates through this
story, "salvation is from the Jews" (4:22), but they will not
accept it in the person of Jesus. Those who accept this salvation
are Samaritans, who are marginalized by the Jews. For them
Jesus "is indeed the Savior of the world" (4:42).

There is no need to detail John's magnificent dramatization
of how a representative of the marginalized Samaritans, "the
Samaritan woman," grew in faith (4:7-26). That has been done
by a host of commentators. What is needful is to note that in
verse 27 the male disciples are shocked that Jesus is talking
with a woman. And there is more shock to come in verses
31-38, which tell of the harvest of "converts" which results
from the preaching of the Samaritan woman turned missionary. Sufficient, however, for our purposes is verse 27: "Just

then his disciples came. They marveled that he was talking with a woman, but none said, 'What do you wish?' or, "Why are you talking with her?'" The observation of Sandra M. Schneiders (1982: 40) sheds considerable light on the meaning of 4:27 in the life situation of the Johannine community:

> It seems more than a little likely that this detail about the disciples being shocked at Jesus' dealing with a woman, since it is in no way necessary to the story itself, is aimed at those traditionalist male Christians in the Johannine community who found the independence and apostolic initiative of Christian women shocking...Jesus alone decides to whom he will reveal himself and whom he will call to apostleship.

Put another way, a person, who is doubly marginalized because she is both a Samaritan and a woman, is presented to us readers as a model of faith and mission. Or as Ben Witherington III (1984: 63) expresses it: "'The hour is coming and now is' when even women, even Samaritan women, even sinful Samaritan women, may be both members and messengers of this King and His Kingdom."

In conclusion, I believe that in this very brief section I have presented adequate evidence on two points. First, Samaritans are people who are marginalized by the Jews because of their geographic origin, among other things. Second, John presents these marginalized Samaritans as readily accepting Jesus as savior of the world. Like the Galilean royal official of 4:43-54 they believe in Jesus' word.

Possible Johannine Life Situation

As we remarked at the end of our lengthy discussion of the Galilean royal official of 4:43-54, it seems that certain marginalized Galileans were members of the Johannine community. With them Jesus shares the opprobrium of being from Galilee (see 1:46). The royal official is representative of their coming to faith in Jesus' word and not in wonders and miracles.

From the story of John 4:4-42 it is easy to draw the inference that the Johannine community has had some success in its mission among the marginalized Samaritans and has retained this story as a record of that mission. If one takes this piece of evidence and combines it with 8:48, further suggestions about the Johannine *Sitz im Leben* may be made. For 8:48 records that Jesus was taunted for being a Samaritan: "The Jews answered him, 'Are we not right in saying that you are a Samaritan and have a demon?'"The sage comment of Wayne A. Meeks (1967: 314) is worth repeating:

> Moreover, as 'Galilean' could be a taunt directed by 'the Jews' against a sympathizer with Jesus (7.52), 'Samaritan' is a taunt hurled at Jesus himself (8.48). Furthermore, while the accompanying taunt, '. . . And you have a demon,' is denied, the accusation that Jesus is a Samaritan is passed over in silence (8.49). Could the Johannine community, or the community in which part of the Johannine traditions were nurtured, have been of such character that Jewish polemics would have included this kind of taunts?

Many scholars have answered Meeks' largely rhetorical question with a loud YES. One of these scholars is Raymond E. Brown (1979: 38) who puts the entry of the Samaritans into the Johannine community in the second phase of his reconstructed history of John's community:

> Accepting these indications, one may posit that the second group in Johannine history consisted of Jews of peculiar anti-Temple views who converted Samaritans and picked up some elements of Samaritan thought, including a christology that was not centered on a Davidic Messiah.

Yes, the Johannine community did include marginalized Samaritans, whom Jesus loved so much that he was willing to be identified with them by name. Jesus, too, was a marginalized Samaritan.

In this chapter it has taken us considerable time to detect another dimension of John's theme of Jesus and the marginalized because we had to probe behind terms of marginalization which were familiar to people at Jesus' and John's times, but strange to us. The time we have spent on John 4 would be comparable to the time it would take us to explain to someone from China the United States meaning of southerner or easterner or Hoosier. I would contend, however, that the time spent has been worthwhile. For it has allowed us to appreciate John's presentation of Jesus going to the geographically marginalized, who willingly accepted him, believing in his word. In their conduct is verified what was announced in the prologue of the Gospel: "He came to his own home, and his own people received him not. But to all who received him, who believed in his name, he gave power to become children of God" (1:11-12).

In the next chapter we will continue our pursuit of a facet of the Johannine theme of Jesus and the marginalized which we touched on momentarily in our treatment of John 4:4-42—Jesus and women.

6

The Women in John's Gospel

Towards the end of the last chapter, in our discussion of the Samaritan woman, we introduced the topic of the role of women in John's Gospel. As you recall, we argued that the Samaritan woman together with her fellow townspeople was marginalized by Judeans because of her geographical origin. And we further indicated in our brief treatments of 4:9 and 4:27 that she was also marginalized because she was a woman and subject to uncleanness. Yet Jesus broke through the barriers of uncleanness and revealed himself to her as the source of life-giving water. And contrary to what one might expect of marginalized people, the Samaritan woman was open to his revelation and even became a missionary of his revelation to her people. Our memories refreshed about what we have already learned concerning the role of women in John's Gospel, it is time now to dedicate an entire chapter to this subject.

Rich Diversity of Models

In our previous chapters the bibliographical fare on our thematic of Jesus and the marginalized in John's Gospel was sparse. The bibliography on the role of women in John's Gospel, however, is a feast: Brown (1979), Collins (1982), Schneiders (1982), Schüssler Fiorenza (1983).

And once we approach the table of this bibliographical feast, we are pleasantly bewildered by the rich diversity of models the authors create to deal with the role of women in John's Gospel. Raymond E. Brown uses the model of an evangelist insisting, at a time when other New Testament churches were proposing "church orders," that what is primary for a Christian is not to have a special ecclesiastical charism, but to have followed Jesus and to be obedient to his word. Women are prime Johannine examples of people who were obedient to Jesus' word. Adela Y. Collins employs the model of a Johannine community whose relationships are characterized by mutuality and not sexist hierarchy. Sandra M. Schneiders works with the model that the Johannine male disciples are reluctant to acknowledge the roles of female disciples in their community; these roles are significant and unconventional. In chapter five above we sampled Schneiders' model in our discussion of John 4:27. Finally, Elisabeth Schüssler Fiorenza argues that John's Gospel provides evidence for her model, namely, Jesus' ministry and communities were characterized by co-equality of discipleship in contrast to the model of patriarchy dominant in Jewish, Greco-Roman, and post-Pauline communities. Her definition of patriarchy is: "While androcentrism characterizes a mind-set, patriarchy represents a social-cultural system in which a few men have power over other men, women, children, slaves, and colonialized people" (1983: 29).

In the face of this rich diversity of models, we might ask about the factors which led to such richness. There seem to be two main factors. First, John's Gospel is unique in the amount of space he gives to and in the stories he tells about women in his Gospel. This fact prompts our authors to ask what in his community situation, theology, and cultural setting led the Fourth Evangelist to give such special roles to women in his Gospel. Second, our four authors, along with many others, are struggling with the contemporary question of the role of women in the church. Implicitly at least, they are asking what God's revelation in John's Gospel might be saying to us in our situation in which women are seeking and assuming greater responsibilities in the church and in which some ecclesiastical communities are not in favor of the ordination of women.

In this chapter I will provide ample samples of these four diverse models as I create my own model. I pursue the following plan. First, I will try to ascertain the facts about the marginalization of women in antiquity. After that I will study the Johannine passages which deal with the Mother of Jesus, Martha and Mary, and Mary Magdalene. Throughout, my model of the situation behind the stories of women in John's Gospel is that of a community inviting Gentile and Jewish women to join it. Through their heroines the Johannine community illustrates to potential converts and to recent converts the roles which women enjoy in their community. In other words, through its picture of women John's Gospel is not so much turned towards opponents in its own community (Schneiders) or towards other Christian communities (Brown and Schüssler Fiorenza) as it is towards bringing into and retaining in the fold women who already confess Jesus as Son of God and Messiah.

The Marginalization of Women in Antiquity

Let us commence with two general statements and then corroborate them from recent research. The first general statement is: it is incorrect to say that in antiquity women had no rights and were inferior to men legally, economically, socially, and religiously. The second generalization is: it is false to make Judaism's view of women so bleak that Jesus' and primitive Christianity's view and praxis are seen as revolutionary and liberating of women marginalized by men and the patriarchical society these men have created.

In giving evidence for my first generalization, I do not call upon New Testament scholars. Rather I turn to Averil Cameron (1980), a classicist who is more directly acquainted with the evidence and whom I will quote extensively. First, Cameron claims that Christianity made little, if any, inroads into the aristocracy, but was successful in its missionary endeavors among the lower and middle-class, whose women were not confined to the home but were active and successful in commercial life:

Already, in fact, in late Republican and early Imperial Rome
large numbers of women of lower and middle-class status
must have lived relatively active lives. As peasant women
no doubt worked in the fields alongside their husbands, so
middle-class women will surely have been associated with
their husband's profession, like St. Paul's Priscilla. We must
assume that the same held for the Greek East. As in many
societies the legal inferiority of women did not prevent them
from leading active lives, while seclusion was normally for
good reason the privilege of the upper class. There is no
good reason, then, to see a basic innovation in the promin-
ence of women among Paul's early converts; they would
have been there naturally in the urban demi-monde in which
Paul moved (1980: 62).

Later on in this excellent article Cameron defines "activity" in
more detail as women's involvement in religious movements:

But women remained marginal in the public life of Rome,
at all social levels, even in the late Republic and early Empire
when a degree of liberation is usually posited for the upper
classes. Even at the highest social level the main method
open to them for exercising power or influence was intrigue,
usually practised from the bedroom. This is not independ-
ence. . . . The major outlet for female activity in the Roman
world (aside from the 'salon culture' available only to the
few) lay in religion, as Roman men, remembering the
Bacchanalian conspiracy, well knew. . . . Clearly Christianity benefited from this pool of available women converts
just as much as rival creeds, and the speed with which
converts were won suggests less a rising status for them in
their social world, or a real new role now offered to them,
than their own lack of public position, which took them to
the mysteries, to Isis, and to Judaism as well as to
Christianity. But once converted to Christianity, they
brought to it the same energy and organizational skill that
many of them employed in their commercial lives (1980:
63).

Finally, Cameron focuses on the marginal nature of the women who were converted to Christianity:

> It (Christianity) belonged naturally to a milieu which by official Roman standards was indeed 'marginal', to say the least. And even when the message was carried beyond the Jewish community proper, its audience was still likely to be found in the lower-middle or middle classes rather than the upper, and among provincials rather than Romans ... in the urban and largely eastern Mediterrean milieu of the early days of Christianity the classes most likely to be reached by Christian preaching were socially and culturally ambiguous ... (1980: 65).

In summary, these extensive quotations from Cameron not only show the truth of our first generalization, but they also demonstrate in what ways women were marginalized in antiquity. In Cameron's terms they lacked "public position" and were, outside of religious sects, unable to exercise power and influence.

Our second generalization about Judaism, Diaspora Judaism in particular, is buttressed by the research of Bernadette J. Brooten (1982). Brooten is persuasive as she argues that synagogue titles given women were not honorific, but real and functional:

> It is my thesis that women served as leaders in a number of synagogues during the Roman and Byzantine periods. The evidence for this consists of nineteen Greek and Latin inscriptions in which women bear the titles 'head of the synagogue,' 'leader,' 'elder,' 'mother of the synagogue' and 'priestess.' These inscriptions range in date from 27 B.C.E. to perhaps the sixth century C.E. and in provenance from Italy to Asia Minor, Egypt and Palestine (1982: 1).

While supporting my second generalization, Brooten's research also corroborates what Cameron has maintained: women would be drawn to religious groups like Judaism and Christianity because it is within them that they could have influence and authority.

In conclusion, these two generalizations and their supporting evidence are not without influence on the model I briefly proposed above about the role of women in John's Gospel. For it is from the research of Cameron and Brooten (and Schüssler Fiorenza: 1983) that I have fashioned the model I stated earlier: when the Johannine community moved into the Diaspora, it encountered women as leaders of Jewish synagogues and converted some of these women leaders. The means of converting these Jewish women leaders and other women were the stories of the heroines of the Johannine community. These stories also offered encouragement to women disciples to persevere in their discipleship. It remains for us to investigate the stories of the Johannine heroines to see how our model makes sense out of them.

The Stories of Women Disciples in John's Gospel

It would be out of place in a book of this brevity to give a detailed exegesis of each of these stories. Sufficient will be observations on how these stories might have appealed to Gentile and Jewish women.

JOHN 2:1-11 and 19:25-27
THE MOTHER OF JESUS

2   On the third day there was a marriage at Cāna in Galilee, and the mother of Jesus was there; [2]Jesus also was invited to the marriage, with his disciples. [3]When the wine failed, the mother of Jesus said to him, "They have no wine." [4]And Jesus said to her, "O woman, what have you to do with me? My hour has not yet come." [5]His mother said to the servants, "Do whatever he tells you." [6]Now six stone jars were standing there, for the Jewish rites of purification, each holding twenty or thirty gallons. [7]Jesus said to them, "Fill the jars with water." And they filled them up to the brim. [8]He said to them, "Now draw some out, and take it to the steward of the feast." So they took it. [9]When the steward of

the feast tasted the water now become wine, and did not know where it came from (though the servants who had drawn the water knew), the steward of the feast called the bridegroom [10]and said to him, "Every man serves the good wine first; and when men have drunk freely, then the poor wine; but you have kept the good wine until now." [11]This, the first of his signs, Jesus did at Cāna in Galilee, and manifested his glory; and his disciples believed in him.

19 [25]But standing by the cross of Jesus were his mother, and his mother's sister, Mary the wife of Clōpas, and Mary Magdalēne. [26]When Jesus saw his mother, and the disciple whom he loved standing near, he said to his mother, "Woman, behold, your son!" [27]Then he said to the disciple, "Behold, your mother!" And from that hour the disciple took her to his own home.

At the beginning of the last chapter we cited the opinion of authors who see a literary and theological pattern in John 2:1-4:54. Moloney (1978: 201), for example, maintains that John 2:1-11 presents Jesus' mother as an example of complete faith in a Jewish context. His is a valuable insight as it highlights the fact that "faith" is a key theme in 2:1-11, especially in 2:5: "Do whatever he tells you." To this insight should be added two others, which the standard commentaries propose. First, Jesus' mother is referred to as "the mother of Jesus" (2:1) and as "woman" (2:4) and is not called "Mary." Through this "strange" terminology the evangelist seems to be moving in the area of the symbolism of expectancy and openness to new life, points to be confirmed by a similar usage of "mother" and "woman" in John 19:25-27. Even the one closest biologically to Jesus, his mother, who as a Jewess expectantly waits for God's fulfillment of messianic promises, must have faith in her son. Not biological ties, but faith is the gate to participation in God's fulfillment of promises during Jesus' hour. Our second insight calls attention to the symbolism of water needed for Jewish rites of purification (2:6) and the new wine of Jesus (2:8-10). It is Jesus, who effects abundant and "the best" wine, and not Jewish rites of purification, who fulfills messianic expectations of abundant life and joy. Thus, this story shows forth in anticipation the messianic gifts which Jesus will bestow when his hour of exaltation arrives. Men and women must approach this Jesus as his mother has—with faith-filled expectation that God will fulfill God's promises in him and during his hour.

This story of the mother of Jesus, faithful disciple of her son, would appeal to women converts. For it showed that one did not have to belong to a particular physical lineage to belong to Jesus' "family." Faith in Jesus is sufficient. Jewish converts would see in Jesus the fulfillment of their fondest messianic expectations. And as we will see below, these Jewish women would not have to give up the leadership roles they were accustomed to exercise in the Jewish synagogues of the Diaspora.

John 19:25-27 is closely related to 2:1-11. Jesus again is present, now as the one who is effecting God's messianic blessings as he goes through his hour of exaltation. His mother as "mother" and "woman" is present. The beloved disciple, the Johannine epitome of discipleship and symbol of Johannine christianity, is also present. Again, the story moves in the realm of symbolism, and rich symbolism at that. In a series of sentences we lay out some of the dimensions of this symbolism. Through his death Jesus has created *a new family*, made up of men and women who have faith in his sovereign power to give life through his death. It is *faith* and not biology which is constitutive of relationships in Jesus' new family. The beloved disciple is now *an adopted child* of Jesus' mother; he is *Jesus' brother* and belongs to Jesus' family: "Woman, behold, your son." And *Jesus' mother has given life* to the beloved disciple, for he is told: "Behold, your mother." Representative of those within Judaism who have carried on the life-giving tradition of Jewish faith and have faithfully waited for God to fulfill God's messianic promises, Jesus' mother gives life to the multi-ethnic Johannine community, represented by the beloved disciple. And both Jesus' mother and the beloved disciple "go home," to start anew and to be "at home" with one another.

In conclusion, prospective Gentile and Jewish converts would see in these stories of Jesus' mother the lesson of faith. It is faith, and not blood line, which determines participation in Jesus' community, a community made up of both men and women, a community in which the choicest blessings God made to Israel are fulfilled, a community in which women, marginalized by their culture, can exercise influence.

JOHN 11:1-12:8
MARTHA AND MARY

11 Now a certain man was ill, Lazarus of Bethany, the village of Mary and her sister Martha. [2]It was Mary who anointed the Lord with ointment and wiped his feet with her hair, whose brother Lazarus was ill. [3]So the sisters sent to him, saying, "Lord, he whom you love is ill." [4]But when Jesus heard it he said, "This illness is not unto death; it is for the glory of God, so that the Son of God may be glorified by means of it."

[5]Now Jesus loved Martha and her sister and Lazarus. [6]So when he heard that he was ill, he stayed two days longer in the place where he was. [7]Then after this he said to the disciples, "Let us go into Judea again." [8]The disciples said to him, "Rabbi, the Jews were but now seeking to stone you, and are you going there again?" [9]Jesus answered, "Are there not twelve hours in the day? If any one walks in the day, he does not stumble, because he sees the light of this world. [10]But if any one walks in the night, he stumbles, because the light is not in him." [11]Thus he spoke, and then he said to them, "Our friend Lazarus has fallen asleep, but I go to awake him out of sleep." [12]The disciples said to him, "Lord, if he has fallen asleep, he will recover." [13]Now Jesus had spoken of his death, but they thought that he meant taking rest in sleep. [14]Then Jesus told them plainly, "Lazarus is dead; [15]and for your sake I am glad that I was not there, so that you may believe. But let us go to him." [16]Thomas, called the Twin, said to his fellow disciples, "Let us also go, that we may die with him."

[17]Now when Jesus came, he found that Lazarus had already been in the tomb four days. [18]Bethany was near

Jerusalem, about two miles off, [19]and many of the Jews had come to Martha and Mary to console them concerning their brother. [20]When Martha heard that Jesus was coming, she went and met him, while Mary sat in the house. [21]Martha said to Jesus, "Lord, if you had been here, my brother would not have died. [22]And even now I know that whatever you ask from God, God will give you." [23]Jesus said to her, "Your brother will rise again." [24]Martha said to him, "I know that he will rise again in the resurrection at the last day." [25]Jesus said to her, "I am the resurrection and the life; he who believes in me, though he die, yet shall he live, [26]and whoever lives and believes in me shall never die. Do you believe this? [27]She said to him, "Yes, Lord; I believe that you are the Christ, the Son of God, he who is coming into the world."

[28]When she had said this, she went and called her sister Mary, saying quietly, "The Teacher is here and is calling for you." [29]And when she heard it, she rose quickly and went to him. [30]Now Jesus had not yet come to the village, but was still in the place where Martha had met him. [31]When the Jews who were with her in the house, consoling her, saw Mary rise quickly and go out, they followed her, supposing that she was going to the tomb to weep there. [32]Then Mary, when she came where Jesus was and saw him, fell at his feet, saying to him, "Lord, if you had been here, my brother would not have died." [33]When Jesus saw her weeping, and the Jews who came with her also weeping, he was deeply moved in spirit and troubled; [34]and he said, "Where have you laid him?" They said to him, "Lord, come and see." [35]Jesus wept. [36]So the Jews said, "See how he loved him!" [37]But some of them said, "Could not he who opened the eyes of the blind man have kept this man from dying?

[38]Then Jesus, deeply moved again, came to the tomb; it was a cave, and a stone lay upon it. [39]Jesus said, "Take away the stone." Martha, the sister of the dead man, said to him, "Lord, by this time there will be an odor, for he has been dead four days." [40]Jesus said to her, "Did I not tell you that if you would believe you would see the glory of God?" [41]So they took away the stone. And Jesus lifted up his eyes

and said, "Father, I thank thee that thou hast heard me. [42]I knew that thou hearest me always, but I have said this on account of the people standing by, that they may believe that thou didst send me." [43]When he had said this, he cried with a loud voice, "Lazarus, come out." [44]The dead man came out, his hands and feet bound with bandages, and his face wrapped with a cloth. Jesus said to them, "Unbind him, and let him go."

[45]Many of the Jews therefore, who had come with Mary and had seen what he did, believed in him; [46]but some of them went to the Pharisees and told them what Jesus had done. [47]So the chief priests and the Pharisees gathered the council, and said, "What are we to do? For this man performs many signs. [48]If we let him go on thus, every one will believe in him, and the Romans will come and destroy both our holy place and our nation." [49]But one of them, Caiaphas, who was high priest that year, said to them, "You know nothing at all; [50]you do not understand that it is expedient for you that one man should die for the people, and that the whole nation should not perish." [51]He did not say this of his own accord, but being high priest that year he prophesied that Jesus should die for the nation, [52]and not for the nation only, but to gather into one the children of God who are scattered abroad. [53]So from that day on they took counsel how to put him to death.

[54]Jesus therefore no longer went about openly among the Jews, but went from there to the country near the wilderness, to a town called Ephraim; and there he stayed with the disciples.

[55]Now the Passover of the Jews was at hand, and many went up from the country to Jerusalem before the Passover, to purify themselves. [56]They were looking for Jesus and saying to one another as they stood in the temple, "What do you think? That he will not come to the feast?" [57]Now the chief priests and the Pharisees had given orders that if any one knew where he was, he should let them know, so that they might arrest him.

12   Six days before the Passover, Jesus came to Bethany, where Lazarus was, whom Jesus had raised from the dead.

²There they made him a supper; Martha served, and Lazarus was one of those at table with him. ³Mary took a pound of costly ointment of pure nard and anointed the feet of Jesus and wiped his feet with her hair; and the house was filled with the fragrance of the ointment. ⁴But Judas Iscariot, one of his disciples (he who was to betray him), said, ⁵"Why was this ointment not sold for three hundred denarii and given to the poor?" ⁶This he said, not that he cared for the poor but because he was a thief, and as he had the money box he used to take what was put into it. ⁷Jesus said, "Let her alone, let her keep it for the day of my burial. ⁸The poor you always have with you, but you do not always have me."

Methodological Concerns

Before investigating the key verses of John 11:1-12:8, we should prepare ourselves to read this passage aright by getting in touch with our tapes and stereotypes (see chapter one). Our passage, especially 11:1-44, is frequently used in the Roman Catholic tradition at wake services and funerals. At these services attention is correctly focused on Jesus' power to raise Lazarus from the dead. And hymns are often sung which stress Jesus as the resurrection and the life. If Roman Catholics have this "funeral" tape playing in their minds when they read 11:1-12:8, they will have a difficult time attending to what our story says about Martha and Mary, especially Martha's confession of faith in 11:27. For them these two women are *just* Lazarus' sisters. So... Get in touch with your tapes.

Even if readers do get in touch with their tapes and dutifully try to hear what our passage is saying about Martha and Mary, their problems are not over. For they are immediately confronted with another set of tapes and stereotypes. This set of tapes feeds in information from Luke's story in 10:38-42 of Martha and Mary. And for Roman Catholics these tapes make hearing what John has to say particularly difficult. For in Roman Catholic circles Luke 10:38-42 is popularly applied to religious life in such a way that Martha is representative of the active life and Mary of the contemplative life. In groups of

Roman Catholic religious men and women one is sure to get at least a few upturned lips when one talks about an individual being a "Martha-Martha" type. But John 11:1-12:8 is not Luke 10:38-42 and surely does not contrast, any more than Luke does, the active and contemplative dimensions of religious life. Let John be John!

In chapter two above we previously discussed John 12:1-8 and what it said about the Johannine community's possession and use of money. We also noted the unique Johannine portrayal of Judas as a greedy person. A caution we raised at that time will be repeated here. Do not harmonize John 12:1-8 with Matt 26:6-13 and Mark 14:3-9, and surely don't harmonize it with Luke 7:36-50. Mary of Bethany is not Mary Magdalene nor is she a prostitute nor is she a public sinner. She is the sister of Martha and Lazarus of Bethany. Let John be John!

Finally, some methodological points which deal specifically with the text of John 11:1-12:8. First, as we mentioned in chapter four above, John 11:1-44 is the seventh of Jesus' signs. And as the seventh, it is the perfect sign, for it depicts Jesus as the giver of life and conqueror of death, the ultimate enemy and power. It should not surprise us that John, in dramatically presenting this perfect sign, gives special billing to some of his important themes, in this instance, the role of women. Second, we should not press the common division of John's Gospel too strongly. This division of chapters 1-12 into the Book of Signs and chapters 13-21 into the Book of Glory should not blind us to the fact that materials in John 11:1-12:8 are related thematically to materials in 13:1-20. Multi-volume commentaries on John's Gospel, like that of Raymond E. Brown, can too easily convey the impression that what is in the Book of Signs is not related to what is in the Book of Glory. As we will see in dealing with the Johannine presentation of Mary of Bethany, that is not the case.

Key Verses in John 11:1-12:8

Space limitations do not permit us the leisure of commenting on every single verse in this large section. The lion's share of our attention will be given to John 11:5; 11:27; 12:2; and 12:3-8.

John 11:5 is deceptively simple: "Now Jesus loved Martha and her sister and Lazarus." Yet once one recalls, along with Brown (1979: 191-92), that discipleship is the primary Christian category for John and that the Johannine disciple par excellence is the disciple Jesus loves, one begins to glimpse the import of 11:5. The Johannine terminology of "to love" (see 3:16; 5:20; 15:15) is similar to one dimension of our word "to love": to love is to share revelation with. One tells the beloved revelations which one doesn't broadcast at the local pub. And the beloved is the one who has received these revelations. Converted into Johannine coinage, this illustration from our own language usage means that Martha, Mary, and Lazarus have been loved by Jesus and have received the revelation of his origin. They are his friends. And once we use "friend," a verbal relative of "to love," we realize further richness in John 11:5. Recall John 15:15: "No longer do I call you servants, for the servant does not know what his master is doing; but I have called you friends, for all that I have heard from my Father I have made known to you." And from within the Johannine tradition additional light is shed on John 11:5 and the meaning of "friend." In 3 John 15 the designation of the Christian is "friend": "Peace be to you. The friends greet you. Greet the friends, every one of them."

It would seem that Gentile and Jewish women, listening to the story of Martha and Mary and Lazarus, would be drawn towards the Johannine community. For its Lord, Jesus, was one who did not reserve his revelation exclusively for men. He loved Martha and Mary as well as Lazarus.

John 11:27 should be viewed in conjunction with 11:24-26. In 11:24 Martha gives voice to Jewish hope in the resurrection. After that, in 11:25-26, Jesus reveals himself as the resurrection and the life and asks whether Martha believes. To this revelation Martha responds: "Yes, Lord; I believe that you are the Messiah, the Son of God, he who is coming into the world." Martha's confession of faith should be, first off, compared with that at the end of John 20: "but these are written that you may believe that Jesus is the Messiah, the Son of God, and that believing you may have life in his name" (20:31). It is obvious that Martha's confession is substantially the same as that of the author of John's Gospel. Both lie at the root of this Gospel. Martha's confession of faith should, secondly, be compared to that of Peter in this Gospel: "You are the Holy One of God" (6:69). Martha's confession is more profound than that of Peter. Thirdly, one should compare Martha's confession with that of Peter in Matt 16:16: "You are the Messiah, the Son of the living God." Now this confession of Peter in Matthew's Gospel is very close to that of Martha's. But what happens when we continue our comparison of Matthew and John? In Matthew, Peter's confession lays the foundation for the church (see 16:17-19). Should we not say the same thing about Martha's confession of faith in John's Gospel? That is, is not her confession of faith the foundation of the Johannine community? Put another way, is not the confession of faith *of a woman* the very foundation of John's church?

Let us take our reflections upon John 11:27 a step further. It is commonly taught by the commentators that the Johannine characters have representative value. That is, they do not merely function historically, but point to dimensions of christian life to be pursued or avoided by the readers. Thus, as we saw in the last chapter, the Samaritan woman is not just a woman who once upon a time chanced upon Jesus, the Jew, but is representative of those outcasts who believe in Jesus' word and lead others to faith in his revelation. Combining this insight about representation with the previous insight about the unique character of Martha's faith, Schneiders (1982: 41) writes:

> Martha appears in this scene as the representative of the believing community responding to the word of Jesus with a full confession of Christian faith. It is a role analogous to Peter's as representative of apostolic faith in Matthew's Gospel. This representative role of Martha is difficult to understand unless women in John's community actually did function as community leaders ... If this confession, given during the public life of Jesus (and recorded in Mat-

thew's Gospel), grounds the promise of the primacy of
Peter, it is no less significant as foundation of community
leadership when given by a woman.

From what I have just said it seems obvious that John 11:27
should not be passed over as we sing our hymns to praise
Jesus, the resurrection and the life. If we have given so much
honor to St. Peter and the rock-like character of his confession
of faith, why have we given so little honor to St. Martha and
her rock-like confession of faith? Surely, it is a disservice to her
faith and to John's Gospel to marginalize her in favor of Peter
and drown her confession out with chants of "Martha, Martha,
you're busy with too many things!"

As I ponder briefly the life situation of John's Gospel in the
light of John 11:27, I repeat one sentence from Schneiders:
"This representative role of Martha is difficult to understand
unless women in John's community actually did function as
community leaders..." Through the story of Martha, especially in John 11:27, the author of John's Gospel was telling
prospective Gentile and Jewish women converts that women
are not marginalized, but are leaders in the Johannine community. In particular, he is telling Jewish women that their
hopes for resurrection have been fulfilled in Jesus, the Messiah,
the Son of God, who is resurrection and life.

John 12:2 is unique to John's Gospel and important; it
should not be skipped over: "There they made him a supper;
Martha served, and Lazarus was one of those at table with
him." As Schneiders (1982: 41-42) suggests, there may be
eucharistic overtones present in this overture to the story of
Jesus' anointing. This supper takes place six days before
Passover. And if one follows the Johannine chronology, this
means that this meal takes place on Sunday, the usual time for
Eucharist in the primitive church. Further, the text says,
"Martha served." The Greek behind this verb is from the same
root (*diakonein*), which stands behind the terms, diakonia and
deacon, to which we immediately give theological significance.
Taking the eucharistic overtones together with this note that
"Martha served," we are led to conclude that more is involved
in Martha's serving than the mere passing around of dishes of

food. In commenting on John 12:2, Brown (1979: 187) makes this excellent point:

> On the story level of Jesus' ministry this (that Martha served) might not seem significant; but the evangelist is writing in the 90s, when the office of *diakonos* already existed in the post-Pauline church (see the Pastorals) and when the task of waiting on tables was a specific function to which the community or its leaders appointed individuals by laying on hands (Acts 6:1-6). In the Johannine community a woman could be described as exercising a function which in other churches was the function of an 'ordained' person.

Martha is model disciple as she serves Jesus and the community.

If we place John 12:2 on the grid of the life situation of John's community, we arrive at these observations. For Gentile and Jewish women interested in joining the Johannine community, the story of Martha in 12:2 contributes another positive element. Martha is not only a representative person because of her confession of faith (11:27), but also because of her ministry at table within the community. Like Martha, these women converts would be able to move from their marginalized situations and "serve" the community.

John 12:3-8 figured prominently in chapter two above, and we need not repeat all of that discussion here. For our purposes, it is sufficient to recall that John 12:3-8 provided us with evidence that Jesus and his disciples used their money to care for the poor.

If we relate John 12:3-8 back to 11:28 and ahead to 13:1-20, we will be the beneficiaries of additional insights into the meaning of 12:3-8. It may have struck you as strange that after Martha uttered a profound christological confession in 11:27, she tells her sister Mary that Jesus the *teacher* is here and is calling for you (11:28). Why "teacher"? Glimmers of an answer are given in 13:5, 13, 14, 15, where "teacher" recurs. Jesus, the teacher, has washed the feet of his disciples and thus given them an example of what it means for them to be disciples: "If

I then, your Lord and Teacher, have washed your feet, you also ought to wash one another's feet" (13:14). Further glimpses of an answer are given by the fact that for disciples to wash their master's feet was an act of veneration. The final rays of an answer are shed by Schneiders' comments: "In Jn 12, Mary anoints her Teacher's feet in an act that resembles (because of her wiping them with her hair) a footwashing. In other words, it seems likely enough that John is deliberately presenting this woman as a disciple of Jesus the Teacher, a role generally forbidden to Jewish women. . ." (1982: 42). What is the evangelist saying to us through these interconnections, some of which may seem subtle to those of us who are accustomed to think that nothing from the Book of Glory relates back to the Book of Signs? Through all this Mary is being presented as the model disciple, who serves Jesus, her teacher, by washing his feet. And her generosity is contrasted with the greed of Judas.

Further insights into the meaning of John 12:3-8 come our way when we recall that many contemporary Johannine scholars view John's community as a "school." In it Jesus is the Teacher, and believers are learners/disciples. From Jesus, especially from his example of washing his disciples' feet, these learners are taught the meaning of discipleship (13:1-20). If this interpretation of John's community as a school is correct, then the evangelist is presenting Mary as a model disciple. For she anticipated Jesus' later example and teaching.

Let us summarize what we have said about Mary of Bethany by reflecting upon her representative role. Mary is representative of the leadership roles which women, as disciples, enjoy in the school of the Johannine community. Potential Gentile and Jewish converts would be attracted to the Johannine community through the story of Mary, the model disciple. For Mary's story shows how it is possible to rise above cultural marginalization and become a disciple of Jesus. The generous spirit, evidenced in her action, is not the prerogative of men. As a matter of fact, one of Jesus' closest disciples, Judas, failed the test of generous service.

CONCLUSION

After these many pages on John 11:1-12:8, a brief summary is in order. Contrary to what our stereotypes and tapes may have said, Martha of Bethany is not busy about many things. And Mary of Bethany is not a public sinner. These women are important figures in John's Gospel. They are loved by Jesus. Martha has foundational faith and is a "deacon" in the community. Mary is generous in her devotion to Jesus, her teacher. The stories of these representative characters would appeal to women outside the Johannine community, for they show how these women have escaped from marginalization and enjoy within the Johannine community the influence of profound faith and generous service.

JOHN 20:1-18
MARY MAGDALENE

20 Now on the first day of the week Mary Māgdalēne came to the tomb early, while it was still dark, and saw that the stone had been taken away from the tomb. [2]So she ran, and went to Simon Peter and the other disciple, the one whom Jesus loved, and said to them, "They have taken the Lord out of the tomb, and we do not know where they have laid him." [3]Peter then came out with the other disciple, and they went toward the tomb. [4]They both ran, but the other disciple outran Peter and reached the tomb first; [5]and stooping to look in, he saw the linen cloths lying there, but he did not go in. [6]Then Simon Peter came, following him, and went into the tomb; he saw the linen cloths lying, [7]and the napkin, which had been on his head, not lying with the linen cloths but rolled up in a place by itself. [8]Then the other disciple, who reached the tomb first, also went in, and he saw and believed; [9]for as yet they did not know the scripture, that he must rise from the dead. [10]Then the disciples went back to their homes.
11 But Mary stood weeping outside the tomb, and as she

wept she stooped to look into the tomb; [12]and she saw two angels in white, sitting where the body of Jesus had lain, one at the head and one at the feet. [13]They said to her, "Woman, why are you weeping?" She said to them, "Because they have taken away my Lord, and I do not know where they have laid him." [14]Saying this, she turned round and saw Jesus standing, but she did not know that it was Jesus. [15]Jesus said to her, "Woman, why are you weeping? Whom do you seek?" Supposing him to be the gardener, she said to him, "Sir, if you have carried him away, tell me where you have laid him, and I will take him away." [16]Jesus said to her, "Mary." She turned and said to him in Hebrew, "Rabbōnī!" (which means Teacher). [17]Jesus said to her, "Do not hold me, for I have not yet ascended to the Father; but go to my brethren and say to them, I am ascending to my Father and your Father, to my God and your God." [18]Mary Māgdalēne went and said to the disciples, "I have seen the Lord"; and she told them that he had said these things to her.

Before we can hear this story properly, we should again check our tapes. In John's Gospel Mary of Magdala is not a sinner. It is Luke's Gospel which has this verse: "Mary, called Magdalene, from whom seven demons had gone out" (8:2). You can search John's Gospel all you want, and you will not find a solitary mention that Mary Magdalene is a sinner. Let John be John!

A more subtle tape is the one which says that women could not be official witnesses. And since they could not be official witnesses, we must see the role Mary Magdalene is given in John 20:11-18 as "unofficial." That is, it's only the witness of the men which counts! But where is the evidence that in the community of Jesus, who transformed Jewish norms, women could not be official witnesses? There is none. Let John be John!

Perhaps, the subtlest tape of them all is the one which says—again and again—Peter is the one! Within the last ten years I have been to St. Peter's in Rome twice and to St. Peter's in the old city of Munich once. Through their statuary, inscriptions, stained glass windows, and high altars these churches proclaimed loud and clear, what our tapes also sing forth, "Peter is the one! There is no other!" The art work hardly had room to acknowledge that Paul was an apostle, let alone someone like Mary Magdalene! But let John be John!

Now that I have once again ridden my hobby horse of "Let John be John," we can commence with our exegetical remarks on John 20:1-8. They will be brief.

The first point to make is that in John's Gospel the risen Jesus appears first to Mary Magdalene. That point must be repeated, for other traditions stress that the risen Jesus first appeared to Peter (see Luke 24:34 and 1 Cor 15:5). One can search through all of John 20 and nowhere find that Jesus appeared first to Peter. The risen Lord has appeared first to one of the marginalized, the woman Mary of Magdala, who herself uses the words of apostolic commission: "I have seen the Lord" (20:18; see 1 Cor 9:1: "Am I not an apostle? Have I not seen Jesus our Lord?"). Readers should let this point sink in and not immediately find comfort in the tape which says that this point doesn't really matter, for she was only an "unofficial witness."

The second point is that Mary Magdalene was given the commission by the risen Jesus to preach the Johannine Gospel. I offer in justification for this point the following brief analysis of 20:17. It is John's good news that Jesus has descended from God to reveal God. Having accomplished this work, he is ascending to his Father. And those who believe that Jesus has accomplished this work become children of God and brothers and sisters of Jesus. Put another way, John 20:17 is a summary of John's entire Gospel; and it is Mary Magdalene's commission to preach this Gospel. And as John 20:18 puts it, she was faithful to her commission.

Our third and final point concerns the terminology for discipleship which pulses through our passage. Once we have become attuned to the nuances of John's Gospel, we will not miss the discipleship term which occurs in John 20:15: "Whom do you *seek*?" In John 1:38 Jesus used this word in addressing the first disciples. Mary Magdalene is presented as a disciple seeking her Lord. The commentators are wont to point out the connection between John 20:16 and John 10:3. Mary Magdalene is indeed one of Jesus' sheep, one of his disciples, who hears his voice and responds to him. And it is not without significance that her response to him is the response of a disciple. She calls Jesus "rabboni" or "teacher" (20:16).

As we conclude this section, we ask: what does this representative figure, Mary Magdalene, contribute to the evangelist's goal of winning over Gentile and Jewish women to his community? First, on the level of discipleship he is saying that discipleship in his community is not limited to men. Women are invited to join. Secondly, leadership roles are open to them, through which they can exercise influence. This is evident from the fact that women like Mary Magdalene enjoyed such an important role during the foundation of the Johannine community. The community will not go back upon its founding vision.

Conclusion and Summary

Our rich bibliographical feast has resulted in the largest chapter in this book. Surely, a summary is appropriate, lest any gems of knowledge escape notice.

Throughout these many pages my points have been three. First, there is an abundance of stories about women in John's Gospel. In stressing the positive role of women in Jesus' mission, John is one with the Synoptics, for as Collins (1982: 52) correctly notes:

> Not only does the gospel of John imply a church where relationships are characterized by mutuality. It suggests one where women are active in the same way as men. In part this is because John shares with *the tradition about Jesus generally* the theme that it is the people of low status who accept the message of Jesus (emphasis mine).

Second, women, who in general were marginalized in antiquity, were able to exercise influence in Judaism and Christianity. Both Diaspora Judaism and Christianity had women leaders. Third and perhaps controversially, the evangelist employed the stories about women to encourage converts. That is, in this chapter I have argued that the evangelist's purpose was missionary and exhortatory rather than apologetic and polemical. He was not concerned to combat the apostolic churches which flew the flag of Peter's leadership. Nor was he concerned to put in their places male chauvinists within his own community. His concern was to be faithful to Jesus' concern for the lowly and thus to bring the good news of Jesus Christ, Son of God, to another group of marginalized—women. Within the Johannine community these marginalized would enjoy co-equality of discipleship with men and would exercise leadership roles. To them Jesus' mother, Martha of Bethany, Mary of Bethany, and Mary of Magdala were heroines and representative of what they were called to be.

7

Nicodemus the Marginalizer
Becomes a Disciple

For five chapters I have been gathering evidence that John's Gospel contains the theme of Jesus and the marginalized. In chapter two we saw that Jesus and his disciples cared for the marginalized poor. Chapter three was taken up with evidence that the religious leaders marginalized those ignorant of the law as "people of the land." These people were drawn to Jesus. In chapter four I explored what John's Gospel had to say about Jesus' ministry to the physically marginalized. And in that chapter we saw the links between chapters four and three as we came face to face with the physically marginalized man-born-blind who was also ignorant of the law and thereby marginalized on that score by the religious leaders. Geographical marginalization was the subject of chapter five, and we noted how both Samaritans and Galileans were marginalized by the Judean religious leaders. Our sixth chapter was dedicated to Jesus' ministry to and with women.

To summarize chapters two to six from another angle, it was often the religious leaders who were responsible for the marginalization. They marginalized the "people of the land," the physically incapacitated, the Samaritans, and the Galileans. Having made this point here, I will leave further development of it to the next chapter. Here I want to ask whether there is any religious leader who breaks the Johannine mold of religious leader as marginalizer. The answer is yes. And his name is Nicodemus.

In this chapter I will build upon the brief comments I made on John 19:38-42 in chapter one above and will argue that Nicodemus is a marginalizer who has become a disciple of Jesus. Put more pointedly, my argument is that Nicodemus is representative of marginalizers who join the community of the marginalized. After arguing my thesis, I will marshal whatever evidence there is for my contention that Nicodemus is also representative of "the rich" who become disciples of Jesus.

Nicodemus, Teacher of Israel, Becomes a Disciple of Jesus

Although our main focus will be on John 19:38-42, we must pick up the clues to the meaning of Nicodemus which John's Gospel provides earlier in the Gospel. Unique to John's Gospel, this "ruler of the Jews" (3:1), this "teacher of Israel" (3:10) does not occur in the Synoptic Gospels. In his first appearance, in John 3:1-15, he is clearly depicted as one of the religious leaders, that is, one who marginalizes "the people of the land" and tells people not to associate with the unclean Samaritans and Galileans. And as we saw in chapter five above in our discussion of John 2:1-4:54, he appears in a sequence of people who come to Jesus. I agree with those commentators who maintain that he has partial faith in Jesus.

Nicodemus reappears in John 7:50-52 in a Johannine trial scene. On trial are Jesus, his message, and his ministry. Those in favor of Jesus are the crowd, whom the religious leaders consider to be ignorant of the law and accursed (see 7:49 and chapter three above). Those against Jesus are the religious leaders. And at the end of this trial Nicodemus, one of the marginalizing religious leaders, is introduced:

> Nicodemus, who had gone to him before, and who was one of them, said to them, 'Does our law judge a man without first giving him a hearing and learning what he does?' They replied, 'Are you from Galilee too? Search and you will see that no prophet is to rise from Galilee.

It seems patent to me that in this passage Nicodemus is moving closer to full faith in Jesus. He has journeyed beyond his secretive coming to Jesus at night. He stands up for Jesus, the marginalized person from Galilee.

The third and final appearance of Nicodemus occurs in the narrative of Jesus' death and burial (19:38-42):

> 38After this, Joseph of Arimathea, who was a disciple of Jesus, but secretly for fear of the Jews, asked Pilate that he might take away the body of Jesus, and Pilate gave him leave. So he came and took away his body. 39Nicodemus also, who had at first come to him by night, came bringing a mixture of myrrh and aloes, about a hundred pounds weight. 40They took the body of Jesus, and bound it in linen cloths with the spices, as is the burial custom of the Jews. 41Now in the place where he was crucified there was a garden, and in the garden a new tomb where no one had ever been laid. 42So because of the Jewish day of Preparation, as the tomb was close at hand, they laid Jesus there.

There are two things that are certain about this text. It is crystal clear that Nicodemus does not occur in the Synoptic accounts of Jesus' burial (Matt 27:57-61; Mark 15:42-47; Luke 23:50-56). There is also great consensus about the enormity of the spices mentioned in verse 39. We are dealing with the Roman pound (roughly twelve ounces). Jesus is buried with eight gallons of spices liquid measure or seventy-five pounds dry measure. In this context I draw my reader's attention to chapter five where in my discussion of the meaning of "royal official" (*basilikos*) I alluded to Josephus, *Jewish Antiquities* XVII.198-99. In that passage Josephus recounts how five hundred servants bore spices at the funeral of King Herod the Great. Jesus' burial is not an ordinary one, but has some of the trappings of a royal burial.

What is one to make of this text about Nicodemus? Commentators are of two opinions. There are those who say that John 19:38-42 is the evangelist's way of saying that Nicodemus has moved from partial faith, to a more firm faith, and finally to complete faith in Jesus as God's revelation. And there are those who champion the view that Nicodemus never rises above a partial faith in Jesus. Paul D. Duke (1985: 110) is representative of those who support this latter viewpoint. He writes:

> "We know that Jesus will be raised; Nicodemus clearly does not... The image evoked is of two remorseful half-disciples sadly piling a mountain of embalming materials onto a body they obviously think is going nowhere. The sound reader, alerted by hyperbolizing imagery (as in 18:3-6), is prompted to leap once more to the post-Easter vantage point of the author. From that height is foreseen a tomb wherein certain lavishly anointed linen cloths lie alone eloquently unnecessary."

Throughout his book Duke has made many insightful observations about the evangelist's use of irony. But I do not think that irony is involved here. First of all, Duke's presentation ignores what seems to be clear: there is a progression of faith in Nicodemus from the account in John 3:1-15 to that in John 7:50-52 and finally to the account under consideration. Further, what Nicodemus does should not be viewed in either-or terms of Jesus' death as one thing and his resurrection as another. In Johannine theology Jesus' death is not to be separated from his resurrection. Thus, Nicodemus' lavishness occurs at Jesus' death which is also Jesus' glorification, that is, his death, resurrection, ascension, and sending of the Spirit. Finally, it is not easy to see how 19:38-42 relates to 18:3-6 and its "hyperbolizing imagery." Even granted that there is some exaggeration in the figure of seventy-five pounds, the perceptive comment of John A.T. Robinson (1985: 283) is well taken: "The Johannine figure, even were it to be exaggerated to bring out the generosity of the gesture, is quite within the bounds of credibility as *a rich man's* last tribute" (emphasis mine).

Representative of those who are of the opinion that the evangelist paints Nicodemus as a believer in John 19:38-42 are Raymond E. Brown (1979: 72 n. 128) and Rudolf Schnackenburg (1982: 295). Brown views these verses in the context of the entire Gospel and writes: "His (Nicodemus') final appearance illustrates the word of Jesus in 12:32-33: 'And when I am lifted up from the earth, I shall draw all men to myself'—this indicated the sort of death he was going to die. " Through his life-giving death Jesus has drawn the religious ruler, the marginalizer, Nicodemus to himself. Schnackenburg interprets the symbolism of the verses themselves, underscoring the royal honor symbolized by the vast amount of spices bought for Jesus' burial. He writes: "In clear contrast to the Jews (v. 31, cf. v. 38) they represent the fellowship of Jesus which shows great honour to its Lord." Schnackenburg's point makes sense to me. As we saw above in our reference to Josephus' account of the burial of King Herod the Great, Jewish royalty was buried with a lavish amount of spices. Moreover, this interpretation of Nicodemus giving Jesus a royal burial is in accord with the theme of Jesus as king which runs through the immediate context of John's Gospel, e.g., 18:36; 19:19-21. In his last vignette about Nicodemus, the religious leader, John portrays him as a disciple of Jesus. Jesus died to draw all people to himself, even those who marginalize the weak.

CONCLUSION

As I come to the end of my reading of John 19:38-42, I deem it helpful to summarize my major points. They have been four. The first is incontrovertible: Nicodemus is a religious leader. John 3:1-15 and 7:50-52 will allow no other interpretation. Secondly, as a religious leader, he belonged to those who marginalized the "people of the land," Samaritans, and Galileans. That point has been argued above, especially in chapters 3-5, and probably will be easily conceded by my readers. My third point is quite controversial. Although the evidence is not as compellingly clear as one might want, there does seem to be sufficient evidence to say that the evangelist completes his portrait of Nicodemus by putting the sign "disciple of Jesus" underneath it. If this is true, then my fourth point follows. The religious leader, Nicodemus the marginalizer, has become a follower of Jesus. He is representative of those marginalizers who have been drawn to Jesus and have joined the Johannine community, a community which is filled with marginalized people.

Nicodemus as a Rich Man

After the above lengthy discussion about Nicodemus as marginalizer joining the community of the marginalized, let me draw out one further point implicit in John 19:38-42. As I read this story, I am quite certain that Nicodemus' generous act of buying seventy-five pounds of spices for Jesus' burial is that of a wealthy man. For, taking guidance from John 12:1-8 wherein the pound of pure nard used to anoint Jesus is valued at three hundred days' wages, I am led to the conclusion that seventy-five pounds of spices can only be afforded by a person of considerable means. Bringing these spices, Nicodemus uses his possessions as his means of showing honor to the one to whom he came in sincere inquiry at night (John 3), the one for whom he stood up when he was being judged unlawfully (7:51), and the one who has finally drawn him to himself in death. Nicodemus' response is not that of rich men in the Synoptics, e.g., Zacchaeus in Luke 19:1-10 or the rich young man in Mark 10:17-31, for he is not called upon to give alms to the poor. Rather, in the Johannine idiom, he is called to have faith in Jesus as the one sent by God. And he expresses that faith, fully grown now, in the generous act of a rich man as he brings a vast amount of spices on behalf of Jesus. His deed is the veneration of a rich man. Let John be John!

Before concluding this section, I will add an apposite, but brief word about the wealth of Joseph of Arimathea. Although some commentators (Lindars 1972: 593; Kysar 1984: 85) maintain that Joseph of Arimathea was wealthy, there is nothing in the text itself nor in its context, immediate or total, nor in Johannine theology which clearly indicates that he was. The Johannine text is not clear that Joseph is the owner of the new tomb in which Jesus is laid. Thus, the new tomb cannot be used as evidence that Joseph was wealthy. It seems that John was more interested in highlighting the actions of one of his own characters, Nicodemus, than in bending the tradition about Joseph of Arimathea in the same direction.

8

John's Life Situation and Ours

In this chapter we have two tasks. One is to draw together the various strands of suggestions about the evangelist's *Sitz im Leben* or life situation which we made in chapters two to seven above. The second is to draw connections between the evangelist's life situation and ours.

The Life Situation of John's Gospel

In chapters two to seven, usually towards the end of the chapter, I made suggestions about the possible life situation behind the evangelist's use of the theme of Jesus and the marginalized. In making these suggestions, I was not only preparing for this chapter in advance, but also was abiding by a sound point in New Testament methodology. That point is this: an evangelist develops a particular theme, not just because it is worthwhile in itself, but because it will nurture the faith life of the community. In gathering together these previous suggestions about life situation, I will make my remarks on two levels. The first shows how my analyses relate to the common opinion about the life situation of John's Gospel. The second will touch on evidence from the Johannine Epistles.

The common opinion about the Johannine *Sitz im Leben* or life situation is that of a Jewish Christian community in conflict with the Jewish synagogue ca. A.D. 90. J. Louis Martyn (1979) has been influential in highlighting John 9:22;

12:42; and 16:2 as key texts for ascertaining this life situation:

> John 9:22: "His parents said this because they feared the Jews, for the Jews had already agreed that if any one should confess him to be Messiah, he was *to be put out of the synagogue*." 12:42: "Nevertheless many even of the authorities believed in him, but for fear of the Pharisees they did not confess it, lest they should be *put out of the synagogue*." 16:2: "They will *put you out of the synagogues*; indeed, the hour is coming when whoever kills you will think he is offering service to God."

Martyn has perhaps gone too far in trying to find a life setting for these instances of "being put out of the synagogues" in the worship service, specifically in the recitation of the Twelfth Benediction of the Eighteen Benedictions. This Twelfth Benediction, which Martyn argues was composed at the time of John's Gospel and mandated to be recited in all synagogues, would have run as follows:

1. For the apostates let there be no hope
2. And let the arrogant government
3. be speedily uprooted in our days.
4. Let the Nazarenes (Christians) and the Minim (heretics) be destroyed in a moment
5. And let them be blotted out of the Book of Life and not be inscribed together with the righteous.
6. Blessed art thou, O Lord, who humblest the proud! (1979: 58).

Martyn surmises from a number of rabbinic passages that "for detecting heretics the Twelfth Benediction was employed in the following manner:

> a. A member of the synagogue does something to arouse suspicion regarding his orthodoxy (cf. John 3:2; 7:52*a*).
> b. The president instructs the overseer to appoint this man to be the delegate of the congregation, i.e., to lead in the praying of the Eighteen Benedictions.

c. Unless the man has a means of avoiding the appointment, he must go before the Ark (Torah Nitch) and recite aloud all of the Eighteen Benedictions, pausing after each to await the congregation's Amen. All listen carefully to his recitation of Benediction number 12.

d. If he falters on number 12, the Benediction Against Heretics, he is removed from his praying.... He is then, presumably, 'drummed out' of the synagogue fellowship (1979: 59-60).

Reuven Kimelman (1981), Ephraim E. Urbach (1981), and Steven T. Katz (1984) have been critical of Martyn's interpretation of John 9:22; 12:42; and 16:2 on a number of points. First, Martyn's reconstruction of the Twelfth Benediction, especially the mention of the "Nazarenes," is not datable to the end of the first Christian century. Second, once "Nazarenes" is eliminated from the earliest form of the Twelfth Benediction, there is no reason to believe that Jewish Christians, publicly reading the word "heretics," would have to include themselves among the heretics and therefore falter in their reading rather than pronounce a curse on their heads. Finally, Martyn's view of matters stresses orthodox confession of faith, which was not much of a concern in Judaism. Rather it was orthopraxy, especially that which upheld the Jewish notion of election, which was of prime concern.

While I am not able to accept the specifics of Martyn's reconstruction of the Johannine life situation, his hypothesis is helpful because it accentuates the polemical character of that situation and will lay the foundation of the hypothesis I now propose. My hypothesis is this: the Jewish Christians of John's community are being threatened with being thrown out of the Jewish synagogue, not because, as Martyn surmises, their belief in Jesus' divinity borders on the heresy of di-theism. Rather they run the risk of being cast out of the synagogue because they believe in a Messiah Jesus, who waters down the "election" of Israel by bringing into God's people the marginalized (Aline M. Steuer 1987). Urbach's critique (1981: 292-93) of Martyn's hypothesis is quite pertinent at this juncture:

While to Christians heresy mainly implied doctrinal dissent, in Judaism doctrinal dissent did not make a Jew into a heretic, a *min*. What made a Jew a heretic was not a slackness in observing the precepts, or even alienation from tradition, but the act of denying the election of the Jews; for that act destroys the conceptual basis on which the separate existence of the Jewish people is founded and endangers its survival. The *minim* (heretics) are treated in the same way as the Samaritans.

Building upon Urbach's observations about election and John's description of Jesus' ministry to the marginalized, I maintain that the religious leaders oppose the Christians of John's community because they perceive them as watering down the standards of election by bringing into their communion Samaritans, and Galileans, the physically incapacitated, the "people of the land," people who are ignorant of the law. The Jewish religious leaders cannot tolerate this view of election and do indeed "drum" the Christians out of the synagogue.

In my hypothetical life situation the stories of Jesus' association with the marginalized have at least two functions. First of all, they demonstrate to the Johannine community the nature of their Messiah Jesus and the origins of their community. Messiah Jesus ministered among the marginalized. As Samuel Rayan (1978) has shown, John's Gospel, from beginning to end, deals with the marginalized. Jesus' public ministry begins and ends with stories of his association with women—his mother in chapter 2 and Martha and Mary in chapter 12. Mary of Magdala is the faithful disciple at the cross and at the tomb. Jesus goes to the physically incapacitated and to the geographically marginalized. He is at home with "the people of the land," those ignorant of the law. And in extending God's revelation to these marginalized people, the Johannine Jesus is described as meeting with severe opposition from the religious leaders. For example, in chapter 9 it is really Jesus and not the man born blind who is on trial before the religious leaders.

The stories of Jesus' dealings with the marginalized also serve as paradigms of behavior for the persecuted members of

John's community. The marginalized are their heroes and heroines. They are strengthened in their dedication to Jesus by the example of Mary. Their missionary endeavors find encouragement in the Samaritan woman and Mary of Magdala. Their patience with the marginalizers may yet bear fruit as the story of Nicodemus illustrates. The story of the man born blind shows that the Father of Jesus will never cast out the person who believes in Jesus. Sharpened by the Johannine polemic against the Jewish synagogue and religious leaders, these stories proclaim that the religious leaders are far from God, and the marginalized are near. Rodney A. Whitacre (1982: 118) aptly expresses this aspect of John's Gospel:

> Those who seem to be so virtuous and who are so sure of their favor in the sight of God are found to be farthest from him. Others who are considered to be distant from God, such as the Samaritan woman and the Herodian official, are found to be open to God, responsive to his revelation when it comes.

There remains one element to integrate into my hypothetical life situation, and that is the Johannine portrayal of Jesus and his disciples using their money to care for the poor. After the Jewish War of A.D. 66-70 and their break with the synagogue, the Johannine community has not thrown overboard all Jewish practices and institutions. It is vitally important that they retain stories of how Jesus and his disciples used their money to care for the poor. As we suggested in chapter two, these poor may be those impoverished by the Jewish War. The Johannine community, like its Lord and Messiah Jesus, will not abandon the poor.

Analyses of the life situation of John's Gospel and the Johannine Epistles by Fernando F. Segovia (1981, 1982a, 1982b, 1982c, 1983, 1985a, 1985b) and by Raymond E. Brown (1982) do not seem to shed significant additional light on the hypothetical life situation I have proposed for John's Gospel. What they do contribute is the insight that "marginalization" continues. But this time it is not Jewish religious leaders who are doing the marginalizing. Now Johannine Christians are marginalizing one another, even to the extent of failing to come to the aid of their poor and starving (see 1 John 3:17).

Our Situation in the Light of John's Situation

In this section I work with another principle which is operative in New Testament interpretation: the community behind a New Testament writing is not much different from a contemporary faith community. Sure enough, they ate differently, had shorter life expectancies, did not travel by car or airplane, and believed that the world was flat. But their problems of faith are the same experienced by us and Christians throughout the century. From their responses to these problems all twentieth century Christians can profit.

Let us deal with christological problems first. José Miranda (1977) may have somewhat overplayed the evidence, but he is surely correct in calling our attention to the fact that one of the Johannine community's major christological problems was the nature of Jesus' Messiahship. Because of our contemporary stress on Jesus' divinity—almost to the downplaying of his humanity—it seems to me that we can too easily bypass the "Messiah" dimension of the Johannine confession of faith in Jesus as both Messiah and Son of God (11:27; 20:31). We say, either explicitly or implicitly, that what counts is that Jesus is "Son of God." His Messiahship is not an important question for us.

But as I have tried to show throughout this book, especially in the first part of this chapter, the question of the nature of Jesus' Messiahship was crucial for the evangelist and his community. Jesus was an "inclusive Messiah," one who came for the marginalized. And in being such a Messiah, he caused the sacred notion of "election" to totter and to crash to the ground. Jesus' followers were "put out of the synagogue" for confessing Jesus as this all-embracing Messiah. Moreover, Jesus did not perform his signs to prove his divinity, but to manifest the Father's love for the marginalized and to demonstrate thereby the nature of his messiahship, a messiah who came for all and not just for the elect. In talking about Jesus' signs, José Comblin (1979: 54-55) is eloquent:

> They were not testimonials to Jesus' divinity but manifestations of the Father's presence. They were not demonstrations of the Father's power but of his love. The signs were acts of resurrection and life that delivered people from weakness and evil to strength and good. The signs show that God speaks to us and that his word is life.

We contemporary Christians may need to sit down with John's Gospel again, acknowledge forthrightly that the christological tape that plays in our minds repeats endlessly "Jesus is Son of God," and begin to revel in Jesus as "inclusive Messiah," who by his words and works revealed God as the God of the marginalized.

Liberation theologians can aid us further in our reflections upon the works of Messiah Jesus. Both Miranda (1977) and Comblin (1979) underscore the importance of John 14:12 in any meditation on the meaning of Jesus in John's Gospel: "Truly, truly, I say to you, the person who believes in me will also do the works that I do; and greater works than these will that person do, because I go to the Father." To be a disciple of Messiah Jesus is to be gifted by the Spirit which Jesus sends once he has returned to the Father. And that gift of the Spirit will prompt those Christians who are open to such promptings to continue the works of Messiah Jesus. And as we have seen in this book, the beneficiaries of these works are the marginalized. And as Miranda (1977: 108) reminds us, the "world" will persecute the followers of Jesus for its works just as they persecuted Jesus for his works:

> Remember, though, that Jesus' miracles were not simply what we call 'good deeds'; they were messianic 'good works.' They implied the terrifyingly revolutionary thesis that this world of contempt and oppression can be changed into a world of complete selflessness and unrestricted mutual assistance. Jesus created an intolerable situation; his behavior and his words were a constant goad to 'the world'; they

inescapably demanded a collective decision. The 'good works' of the Messiah did not consist in giving what was left over, in distributing the surplus of a civilization that in itself remains untouched by the distribution. They were not works of supererogation. Had they been no more than that, Christ would not have been afraid nor would he have died as he did.

A final reflection upon a Messiah who ministered to the marginalized is that this Messiah himself became marginalized. He had identified himself so much with the marginalized that he himself was thrown out of the synagogue. And then condemned by both religious and political authorities, he became, as the crucified, the symbol of all marginalized people.

What John's Gospel has to say about the marginalized themselves speaks a challenging word to us today. The stereotype one readily carries of the marginalized person is that this person has no depth, is mean, self-centered, and humanly unlikeable. This stereotype does not hold water as one reflects upon John's Gospel. Take, for instance, the Samaritan woman, who can be too quickly assimilated to our contemporary stereotype of the mindless loose woman. And yet our brief analysis in chapter five above indicated that she had a depth of soul. Men and women, like the Samaritan woman, did not become the heroes and heroines of the Johannine community because they were weak and morally lamentable people. How often do we keep the marginalized in their places by our stereotypes?

Very much in place at this time is a reflection upon the role of women in John's Gospel and in our society and churches. As we saw in chapter six above, Messiah Jesus went out to women in their marginalization. And women enjoyed significant leadership roles in John's community. We may live in a different era, but the marginalization of women continues apace. In some ecclesiastical communities major leadership roles are consistently denied women. And it is frightening to read a book like Ruth Sidel's *Women and Children Last: The Plight of Poor Women in Affluent America* (1987). For us followers of Jesus the Messiah, in affluent America, we need to hear again the story of Jesus' love, concern, and messianic works for marginalized women.

As a final reflection upon John's situation and ours, I would invite my readers back to my Introduction, especially to the excursus at its end. The statements of the ecclesiastical bodies quoted in that excursus make eminent sense in the light of the testimony of John's Gospel, for this Gospel, too, proclaims loud and clear that peace and justice, especially for the marginalized, are a constitutive element of the Gospel. John's Gospel gives no comfort and support to those who out of hand condemn liberation theology.

Conclusion

As I said in my Introduction, this book belongs to the genre of "questions-to-be-disputed." In it I have relentlessly argued a single point: the theme of Jesus and the marginalized exists in John's Gospel. After setting forth the methods I would use and the cautions I would invoke, I went about my argument chapter by chapter. In this chapter I have summarized my materials from two perspectives: John's situation and ours. If my book has prompted you to re-read and re-study John's Gospel, praise the Lord! If I have given you reason to re-examine your previous views on John's Gospel, I am grateful. If I have persuaded you of my position, welcome aboard.

Selected Bibliography

Ashton, John (ed.)
1986   The Interpretation of John. Issues in
                    Religion and Theology 9; Philadelphia:
                    Fortress Press.

Barrett, C.K.
1978   The Gospel According to St. John. 2nd ed.
                    Philadelphia: Westminster Press.

Bauer, Walter
1912   Das Johannesevangelium. Handbuch zum
                    Neuen Testament II, 2; Tübingen: Mohr.

Becker, Jürgen
1986   "Das Johannesevangelium in Streit der
                    Methoden (1980-1984),"Theologische Rund-
                    schau 51:1-78.

Bogart, John
1977   Orthodox and Heretical Perfectionism in
                    the Johannine Community as evident in the
                    First Epistle of John. Society of Biblical
                    Literature Dissertation Series 33; Missoula:
                    Scholars Press.

Brooten, Bernadette J.
1982   Women Leaders in the Ancient Synagogue:
                    Inscriptional Evidence and Background Is-
                    sues. Brown Judaic Studies 36; Chico: Scho-
                    lars Press.

Brown, Raymond E.
1966   The Gospel According to John (I-XII).
                    Anchor Bible 29; Garden City: Doubleday.

Brown, Raymond E.
1970   The Gospel According to John (XIII-XXI).
                    Anchor Bible 29A; Garden City: Double-
                    day.

Brown, Raymond E.
1979   *The Community of the Beloved Disciple.*
               New York: Paulist Press.
Brown, Raymond E.
1982   *The Epistles of John.* Anchor Bible 30;
               Garden City: Doubleday.
Bultmann, Rudolf
1971   *The Gospel of John: A Commentary.*
               Oxford: Blackwell.
Cameron, Averil
1980   "Neither Male Nor Female," *Greece &
               Rome* 27: 60-68.
Collins, Adela Yarbro
1982   "New Testament Perspectives: The Gospel
               of John," *Journal for the Study of the Old
               Testament,*" 22: 47-53.
Comblin, José
1979   *Sent from the Father: Meditations on the
               Fourth Gospel.* Maryknoll: Orbis Press.
Culpepper, R. Alan
1983   *Anatomy of the Fourth Gospel: A Study in
               Literary Design.* Philadelphia: Fortress
               Press.
Danby, Herbert
1933   *The Mishnah.* London: Oxford University
               Press.
Davies, W.D.
1964   *The Setting of the Sermon on the Mount.*
               Cambridge: Cambridge University Press.
de Jonge, Marinus
1977   *Jesus: Stranger from Heaven and Son of
               God.* Society of Biblical Literature Sources
               for Biblical Study 11; Missoula: Scholars
               Press.
Duke, Paul D.
1985   *Irony in the Fourth Gospel.* Atlanta: John
               Knox.

Dunn, James D.G.

1983   "Let John be John: A Gospel for Its Time."
       pp. 309-339 in Peter Stuhlmacher (ed.), *Das
       Evangeliem und die Evangelien: Vorträge
       vom Tübinger Symposium 1982.* Wissen-
       schaftliche Untersuchungen zum Neuen
       Testament 28; Tübingen: Mohr.

Epstein, I. (ed.)

1938   *The Babylonian Talmud.* London: Soncino
       Press.

Finkelstein, Louis

1962   *The Pharisees: The Sociological Back-
       ground of Their Faith.* 2 vols. 3rd rev. ed.
       Philadelphia: Jewish Publication Society of
       America.

Fiorenza, Elisabeth Schüssler

1983   *In Memory of Her: A Feminist Theological
       Reconstruction of Christian Origins.* New
       York: Crossroad.

Fitzmyer, Joseph A.

1981   *The Gospel According to Luke (I-IX).*
       Anchor Bible 28; Garden City: Doubleday.

Fortna, Robert T.

1974   "Theological Use of Locale in the Fourth
       Gospel," *Anglican Theological Review*,
       Supplement Series 3:58-95.

Freyne, Seán

1980   *Galilee From Alexander the Great to
       Hadrian 323 B.C.E. to 135 C.E.: A Study
       of Second Temple Judaism.* Wilmington:
       Glazier; Notre Dame: University of Notre
       Dame Press.

Giblin, Charles H.

1980   "Suggestion, Negative Response, and Posi-
       tive Action in St John's Portrayal of Jesus
       (John 2.1-11; 4.46-54; 7.2-14; 11.1-44)," *New
       Testament Studies* 26:197-211.

Haenchen, Ernst
1984   *John 1 and 2*. Hermeneia; Philadelphia: Fortress Press.

Hoehner, Harold W.
1972   *Herod Antipas*. Society for New Testament Studies Monograph Series 17; Cambridge: Cambridge University Press.

Hoskyns, Edwyn C.
1940   *The Fourth Gospel*. Ed. Francis Noel Davey. London: Faber and Faber.

Katz, Steven T.
1984   "Issues in the Separation of Judaism and Christianity after 70 C.E.: A Reconstruction," *Journal of Biblical Literature* 103: 43-76.

Kimelman, Reuven
1981   "*Birkat Ha Minim* and the Lack of Evidence for an Anti-Christian Jewish Prayer in Late Antiquity." pp. 226-244; 391-403 in E.P. Sanders (ed.), *Jewish and Christian Self-Definition, Vol. 2: Aspects of Judaism in the Graeco-Roman Period*. Philadelphia: Fortress Press.

Kysar, Robert
1983   "The Gospel of John in Current Research," *Religious Studies Review* 9: 314-323.

Kysar, Robert
1985   "The Fourth Gospel. A Report on Recent Research." pp. 2389-2480 in Hildegard Temporini and Wolfgang Haase (eds.), *Aufstieg und Niedergang der römische Welt*, II, 25, 3. Berlin: de Gruyter.

Kysar, Robert
1986   *John*. Augsburg Commentary on the New Testament. Minneapolis: Augsburg.

Lindars, Barnabas
1972   *The Gospel of John*. New Century Bible; London: Oliphants.

Malina, Bruce J.
1985   *The Gospel of John in Sociolinguistic Perspective.* Center for Hermeneutical Studies in Hellenistic and Modern Culture, Colloquy 48. Berkeley.

Martyn, J. Louis
1979   *History & Theology in the Fourth Gospel.* Rev. ed. Nashville: Abingdon Press.

McPolin, James
1982   *John.* rev. ed. New Testament Message 6; Wilmington: Michael Glazier.

Mead, A.H.
1985   "The *basilikos* in John 4.46-53," *Journal for the Study of the New Testament* 23: 69-72.

Meeks, Wayne A
1966   "Galilee and Judea in the Fourth Gospel," *Journal of Biblical Literature* 85: 159-169.

Meeks, Wayne A.
1967   *The Prophet-King: Moses Traditions and the Johannine Christology.* Supplements to Novum Testamentum 14; Leiden: Brill.

Miranda, José Porfirio
1974   *Marx and the Bible: A Critique of the Philosophy of Oppression.* Maryknoll: Orbis Press.

Miranda, José Porfirio
1977   *Being and the Messiah: The Message of St. John.* Maryknoll: Orbis Press.

Moloney, Francis J.
1978   "From Cana to Cana (John 2:1-4:54) and the Fourth Evangelist's Concept of Correct (and Incorrect) Faith." pp. 185-213 in E. A. Livingstone (ed.), *Studia Biblica 1978, II.* Journal for the Study of the New Testament, Supplement Series 2; Sheffield: JSOT Press.

Moulton, J. H.; Milligan, G.
1915   *The Vocabulary of the Greek Testament Illustrated from the Papyri and Other Non-Literary Sources.* London: Hodder and Stoughton.

O'Day, Gail R.
1986   *Revelation in the Fourth Gospel: Narrative Mode and Theological Claim.* Philadelphia: Fortress Press.

Oppenheimer, Aharon
1977   *The 'Am Ha-Aretz: A Study in the Social History of the Jewish People in the Hellenistic-Roman Period.* Arbeiten zur Literatur und Geschichte des hellenistischen Judentums 8; Leiden: Brill.

Pancaro, Severino
1975   *The Law in the Fourth Gospel.* Supplements to Novum Testamentum 42; Leiden: Brill.

Prete, Benedetto

1978   "I poveri' nel racconto giovanneo dell' ungione di Betania (Giov. 12, 1-8).' pp. 429-444 in Associazione Biblica Italiana (ed.), *Evangelizare pauperibus.* Atti della XXIV settimana biblica; Brescia: Paideia.

Rayan, Samuel
1978   "Jesus and the poor in the Fourth Gospel,' *Biblebhashyam* 4: 213-228.

Robinson, John A. T.
1985   *The Priority of John.* London: SCM Press.

Schnackenburg, Rudolf
1968   *The Gospel According to St. John.* Vol 1: Chaps. 1-4. New York: Herder.

Schnackenburg, Rudolf
1980   *The Gospel According to St. John.* Vol. 2: Chaps. 5-12. New York: Seabury.

Schnackenburg, Rudolf
1982   *The Gospel According to St. John.* Vol 3: Chaps. 13-21. New York: Crossroad.

Schneiders, Sandra M.
1982   "Women in the Fourth Gospel and the Role of Women in the Contemporary Church," *Biblical Theology Bulletin* 12: 35-45.

Segovia, Fernando F.
1981   "The Love and Hatred of Jesus and Johannine Sectarianism," *Catholic Biblical Quarterly* 43: 258-272.

Segovia, Fernando F.
1982a   "John 13:1-20, The Footwashing in the Johannine Tradition," *Zeitschrift für die Neutestamentliche Wissenschaft* 73: 31-51.

Segovia, Fernando F.
1982b   *Love Relationships in the Johannine Tradition: Agape/Agapan in I John and the Fourth Gospel.* Society of Biblical Literature Dissertation Series 58; Chico: Scholars Press.

Segovia, Fernando F.
1982c   "The Theology and Provenance of John 15:1-17," *Journal of Biblical Literature* 101: 115-128.

Segovia, Fernando F.
1983   "John 15:18-16:4a—A First Addition to the Original Farewell Discourse?" *Catholic Biblical Quarterly* 45: 210-230.

Segovia, Fernando F.
1985a   "The Structure, Tendenz, and Sitz im Leben of John 13:31-14:31," *Journal of Biblical Literature* 104: 471-493.

Segovia, Fernando F.
1985b   "Peace I Leave with You; My Peace I Give to You': Discipleship in the Fourth Gospel." Pp. 76-102 in Fernando F. Segovia (ed.). *Discipleship in the New Testament.* Philadelphia: Fortress Press.

Sidel, Ruth
1987   *Women and Children Last: The Plight of Poor Women in Affluent America.* New York: Penguin Books.

Smalley, Stephen S.
1978   *John: Evangelist and Interpreter.* Exeter: Paternoster Press.

Smalley, Stephen S.
1986   "Keeping up with Recent Studies XII. St. John's Gospel," *Expository Times* 97: 102-108.

Sobrino, Jon
1984   *The True Church and the Poor.* Maryknoll: Orbis Press.

Stählin, G.
1964   *"Asthenes, ktl."* Pp. 490-493 in *Theological Dictionary of the New Testament* 1. Grand Rapids: Eerdmans.

Steuer, Aline M.
1987   "Some Implications of Social History on the Divisions of the Johannine Community." M.A. Thesis. Chicago: Catholic Theological Union.

Strack, Hermann; Billerbeck, Paul
1922   *Kommentar zum Neuen Testament aus Talmud und Midrasch.* Vol. 1. Munich: Beck.

Strack, Hermann, Billerbeck, Paul
1924   *Kommentar zum Neuen Testament aus Talmud und Midrasch.* Vol. 2. Munich: Beck.

Urbach, Ephraim E.
1975   *The Sages: Their Concepts and Beliefs.* 2 vols. Jerusalem: Magnes Press.

Urbach, Ephraim E.
1981   "Self-Isolation or Self-Affirmation in Judaism in the First Three Centuries: Theory and Practice." pp. 268-298; 413-417 in *Jewish and Christian Self-Definition, Vol. 2: Aspects of Judaism in the Graeco-Roman Period.* Philadelphia: Fortress Press.

Weir, J. Emmette
1986   "Liberation Theology Comes of Age," *Expository Times* 98: 3-9.

Whitacre, Rodney A.
1982   *Johannine Polemic: The Role of Tradition and Theology.* Society of Biblical Literature Dissertation Series 67; Chico: Scholars Press.
Witherington, Ben
1984   *Women in the Ministry of Jesus: A Study of Jesus' Attitudes to Women and their Roles as Reflected in His Earthly Life.* Society for New Testament Studies Monograph Series 51; Cambridge: Cambridge University Press.

Since this manuscript was completed, only one significant study on its thematic has been published. See David Rensberger, *Johannine Faith and Liberation Community.* Philadelphia: Westminster Press, 1988, especially chapters six and seven.